LIVING ON
FLOOD PLAINS
AND WETLANDS

ALSO BY MAUREEN GILMER:

The Complete Guide to Southern California Gardening
The Complete Guide to Northern California Gardening
California Wildfire Landscaping

LIVING ON FLOOD PLAINS AND WETLANDS

A HOMEOWNER'S HIGH-WATER HANDBOOK

Maureen Gilmer

Taylor Publishing Company
Dallas, Texas

Published by Taylor Publishing Company
        1550 West Mockingbird Lane
        Dallas, Texas 75235

Designed by Hespenheide Design

Library of Congress Cataloging-in-Publication Data

Gilmer, Maureen.
        Living on flood plains and wetlands : a homeowner's high water handbook / Maureen Gilmer.
            p.   cm.
        Includes bibliographical references.
        ISBN 0-87833-887-X
        1. Dampness in buildings. 2. Flood plains. 3. Wetlands.
    I. Title.
    TH9031.G53   1995
    693'.892—dc20   94-42174
                                                          CIP

Published in the United States of America

10 9 8 7 6 5 4 3 2 1

TO ALL MY FRIENDS AT

MHM, Inc.
Engineers and Surveyors Since 1892

Marysville, California,

at the confluence of the Yuba and Feather rivers.

Special thanks to

John Michael Smith, PE
Edgar Hanlin, LS
Donald Solheim, LS
Roger Hanlin, LS

and the MHM staff:

Joanne Kolar
Rosemary Gregg
Trina Fellner
Charlie de St. Maurice
Karna-lisa Aucoin
Jim Miller

My heartfelt appreciation to Holly McGuire,
my efficient, gentle, and always supportive editor.

CONTENTS

INTRODUCTION

Water is unquestionably one of the vital keys to our future security and survival, as well as our well-being. If this nation is to end the waste of our water resources, if we are to develop more fully the use of our water for economic growth and the needs of our exploding population, we should—without further delay—greatly accelerate our programs as regards conservation, transportation, power, flood control, and other aspects of our natural water resources.

John F. Kennedy

The story of our American waterways begins hundreds of years ago, when pioneers wandered through a virgin land where nature reigned supreme. Tiny, fledgling populations could do little more than simply flee to high ground when tempestuous waters periodically inundated towns and farms. Over time the cities grew up; new concerns such as improved navigation, increased commerce, water resource development, and, perhaps best known of all, human safety guided the hands of governments.

The U.S. Army Corps of Engineers took on the task of organizing waterway improvement projects on a national basis in order to attain the modern goals of navigation and flood control. Among its greatest achievements were hydroelectric dams, flood control facilities, bridges, vast levee systems, and many other mechanical means of controlling rivers and coastal waterways. But despite its best efforts, disastrous flooding continued as development encroached onto the flood plain and sometimes into the floodway itself.

By the 1960s a broader approach to flood control was implemented, using land use regulation, better flood forecasting, federal flood insurance, and even relocating property out of the floodway to reduce damage. The Corps set its efforts to developing flood data for entire watersheds and river basins in order to determine suitable land uses that would not increase the flooding potential. It was indeed a time of transition.

During the environmental decade of the 1970s, new laws concerning plants and wildlife brought an added dimension to the Corps's responsibilities. This was no easy matter because the Corps was staffed with civil engineers trained in large-scale, mechanical flood control methods. Yet they were

I

now charged with issues of pollution, watershed management, status of wetlands in their myriad forms, and care of groundwater aquifers. Many of the engineers found it difficult to make the transition and to learn new ways of working with other professions concerned with environmental quality.

As the progressive 1980s arrived, the emphasis was on coastal conditions, where development was actively curtailed by regulatory agencies concerned by offshore drilling, dune destabilization, and displacement of coastal habitat by homes and commercial waterfront marinas. The Corps and other agencies continued to evolve from problem solving to regulatory enforcement of the tremendous number of new federal programs controlling the use of waterways and flood plains. The following are just some of the many examples of legislation that went into effect between 1960 and 1990. They illustrate just how massive a web of regulations the Corps must contend with and how challenging its task will be in years to come.

Housing Act of 1961
Land and Water Conservation Fund Act, 1964
National Flood Insurance Act, 1968
National Environmental Policy Act, 1969
Coastal Zone Management Act, 1972
Clean Water Act of 1972
National Dam Inspection Act of 1972
Endangered Species Act of 1973 '
Flood Disaster Protection Act of 1973
Disaster Relief Act of 1974
Federal Land Policy and Management Act of 1976
Housing and Community Development Act of 1977
Coastal Barrier Resources Act, 1982
Dam Safety Act, 1986
Emergency Wetlands Resources Act of 1986
Water Resources Development Act, 1986
Housing and Urban Development Act of 1987
Disaster Relief and Emergency Assistance Amendments of 1988
Executive Order 11990, Protection of Wetlands
Water Resources Development Act of 1990

Combined with new regulations concerning environmental issues of the 1990s, such as new clean water legislation, it is clear that there are big changes in the roll of the Corps of Engineers. Similar changes have also come about in the USDA Soil Conservation Service, which is heavily involved with wetland identification on private agricultural lands. Yet despite the increased responsibility, these agencies are suffering from declining budgets and limited staff.

We must all understand that the turn of this new century will bring many changes and much frustration all around as we seek to balance the needs of individual citizens with those of the environment and our economy. Many debatable theories of emerging environmental science are today being accepted as law, which becomes dangerous when they are the basis for regulating property owners' rights and land use. In our zealous effort to protect the ecology, it is easy to make mistakes that can have far-reaching consequences into the future. And in the long run, it is the survival of the family as a viable economic unit that determines whether we will continue to grow and prosper as a nation.

This book was written to give people the tools they need to deal with flooding and the potential for more frequent flooding in the future. It also attempts to show how America's goals are changing and that few issues are as cut and dried as they used to be. Some issues of the environment are of true concern, but they can also become political tools rife with hidden agendas and power plays. Only in the midst of disasters such as the flooding of the Mississippi, the recent high water of the southeastern states, and the flooding in Houston, Texas, do the truths come to light. It is clear that above all, floods kill people, and there is nothing more important to Americans living in and among our wetlands and flood plains.

"Love this river, stay by it, learn from it." Yes, he wanted to learn from it, he wanted to listen to it. It seemed to him that whoever understood this river and its secrets, would understand much more, many secrets, all secrets.
Hermann Hesse

I
HISTORIC FACTS CONCERNING WETLANDS AND FLOOD PLAINS

On that day all the springs of the great deep burst forth, and the
floodgates of the heavens were opened. And rain fell on the earth
for forty days and forty nights.

Genesis 7:11

Humans have always made their homes beside waterways, which provided food, drink, irrigation, transportation, and the myriad other benefits of civilization. Mesopotamia, the verdant land between the Tigris and Euphrates rivers of the Middle East, was a cradle of civilization. Without water there can be no life, but where it is plentiful, the land is fertile and life springs forth in great abundance.

Perhaps the best example of this is Africa's Nile River, which overflowed its Egyptian banks since the beginning of time. Aerial views reveal an endless barren desert through which meanders the river channel, flanked by strips of green. Before the Aswan and other dams regulated the Nile's flow, the waters would swell over their downstream banks with the rainy season upstream, carrying fertile silt to blanket the land in new earth after the water receded. This seasonal flooding is what made the fields of the Egyptians produce enough to feed a whole civilization amidst an arid wasteland. Without that river there would be no pyramids or pharaohs, and even more of the land that is Egypt would be a barren desert.

Some of the first reports of America's great rivers came from De Soto's struggle to explore North America. In 1539 the party became the first Europeans to witness a seasonal flood on the Mississippi. Garcilaso de la Vega wrote that the water "overflowed the wide level ground between the river and the cliffs that loomed some distance away; then, little by little it rose to the top of the cliffs. Soon it began to overflow the meadows in an immense flood." During this time they realized the Native Americans were well prepared for such an event, with their villages perched upon dry hills or manually created mounds to keep above the water.

This aerial view shows the very wide, flat topography that characterizes our low-land flood plains. (California Department of Water Resources)

When the early American pioneers began to make their way westward from the east coast, they encountered many great waterways. On these conduits traveled the Native Americans and the first French *voyageurs* in their birch bark canoes. Later the flatboats carried settlers effortlessly to their new homes, for it was far easier to float downstream than it was to walk those miles. With travel dependent upon rivers, riverbank settlements sprang up and later became great cities like Cincinnati, St. Louis, Memphis, and Kansas City.

The histories of these cities are filled with destructive floods because the rivers would rise during seasons of heavy rainfall. The towns and surrounding farms were inundated, the residents forced to flee to high ground and later to suffer the inevitable famines from lost crops in the bottomlands. Yet the settlements were rebuilt because of their strategic locations along rivers of commerce.

The water in a flooded river would fan out over a very large area called a flood plain. The greater the volume of water flowing in the river, the farther it would wander from the main channel. Originally river flooding was not as catastrophic as today because 1) human populations in flood plains were smaller, 2) runoff was checked by vegetation, 3) overflow gathered in lowlands, and 4) no artificial obstructions increased depth before overflow.

A river would remain in a flooded state for weeks at a time, and its slow flow caused minimal erosion, the sediment gathered upstream gradually drop-

Mississippi Watershed.

ping out along the flood plain. Once the flood plain again surfaced, the land was enriched and fertile, making this some of America's most coveted agricultural soils.

AMERICA'S GREAT WATERSHEDS

The term **watershed** applies to the area draining into a river or basin. In the case of the Mississippi River watershed, America's largest, this single drainage is fed by other large rivers and streams in 31 states and 2 Canadian provinces. This watershed covers 1.25 million square miles, which explains why so many historic floods and flood control efforts are centered on this single waterway. From the source of the Mississippi at Lake Itaska in Minnesota to St. Louis, Missouri, the river is more irregular and carries a smaller volume of water. From St. Louis south to New Orleans at the Delta, the Mississippi is joined by the Missouri, Ohio, Arkansas, and Red Rivers to produce a vast amount of water funneled down through Louisiana.

It is not difficult to understand why weather events in the northern states can have disastrous effects by the time the Mississippi enters the South. The runoff from its more than 100,000 tributaries carries a great deal of soil and organic matter. Originally the landscape was well vegetated with forests and thick prairie grass sod, both of which acted much like sponges. The vegetation could absorb a tremendous amount of water and filter the runoff, catching sediment before it reached the main channel. But as farmers settled the prairie, they stripped off this protective layer of sod in order to expose the earth, a practice that would later contribute to extreme erosion in the prairie states. In modern times the further development of cities and residential areas has caused even more land to be paved, eliminating any possibility of rainfall absorption into the soil and further increasing runoff.

With sod and forests, two of nature's most effective flood control mechanisms, reduced in area, increased runoff ran unchecked and unfiltered through the watershed. Unfortunately, the sediment load also poured into the rivers, where the silt dropped out, filling channels and thus reducing capacity. The combination of shallower channels, increased water velocity, and additional runoff forced the flood plain to become wider in order to accommodate the flood waters, which inundated more and more of the arable land.

The Changes in American Watershed Status

Time period	Absorption	Runoff
Pre-settlement	Maximum	Minimum
Settlement	Minimum	Increased
Urban-Suburban	None	100%

THE ADVENT OF LEVEES

As the cities grew, the demand rose for some sort of flood control. One of the first to utilize active flood control was the French city of New Orleans, where the mighty Mississippi River rose and fell with the seasons and parts of the city were often underwater. Inundation there caused serious problems with waterborne diseases such as cholera. Protecting the city was essential if epidemics were to be controlled. The solution was the **earthen levee**: a mass of compacted soil that acted as a dam and extended around low, vulnerable parts of the city to keep the waters at bay.

Human settlement of the North American heartland created more watershed runoff and a greater burden to the waterways. With flood waters growing higher each year due to increased water volume and more shallow channels, the need for protecting cities and suburbs increased. Levees and floodwalls were built along the rivers and at strategic places in the countryside in order to protect communities with a barrier system.

When rivers are constrained by levees on both banks, the water level will rise as a greater volume is forced between the barriers. For example, an unaltered river in a flooded state spreads out at a depth of 1 foot for a distance of 1,000 feet on either side of the main river channel. That same volume of water if contained between two levees may rise 20 feet because it is not permitted to fan out in a **normal flood event**. As a result the water flows faster and much deeper. Its surface elevation is also 20 feet above the surrounding plain. Should the levee break, the water would flow out through the gap like a tidal

Rivers which once wandered all over the flood plain are now constrained by levees. Here are the two most common reasons for building levees: to create more farm land and to allow residential development. These homes have only this ribbon of levee to protect them in times of high water, which can reach the very top of these levees. In fact, the Corps of Engineers has recommended that these levees be raised another 18 inches to accommodate increased flows. (California Department of Water Resources)

wave, a scenario referred to as flash flooding, although in this case part of an overall flood. These waves can be powerful enough to tear buildings from their foundations and whisk away heavy equipment. Serious damage occurs during flash flooding caused by breaks in levees and dams where great volumes of water have been impounded.

How Levees Fail

With levees built along many American waterways during the nineteenth and twentieth centuries, most of our rivers are heavily constrained within relatively narrow channels. Levees are often effective in controlling flooding, but as many saw during the summer of 1993, long-term rainfall coupled with very high flood water can be too much for them. Once the soil mass of a levee becomes completely saturated, its structural integrity is threatened and sometimes impossible to repair.

In many communities the levee systems evolved over a century or more, some privately owned and others built by the government. Often levees were begun as smaller embankments built by hand, with horse and wagon moving soil from nearby borrow pits to create the berms. In many cases there was little

This aerial shows the remnants of a levee that failed, and water is flowing into the surrounding lowlands at such speed it exhibits a noticeable rippling effect. The bridge in the background has lost a span, which is usually caused by large debris slamming into the pilings. (California Department of Water Resources)

thought given to the type of soil used or to the quality of ground the levee was being built upon. Over time the levees were raised, rebuilt, and repaired periodically, as funds and needs allowed. Some are a sandwich of many different layers hidden beneath a top covering that is well packed and graded. Wherever these

WHO ARE TODAY'S U.S. ARMY CORPS OF ENGINEERS?

In most communities there is an ongoing effort to repair and maintain the levee systems. This is controlled by the U.S. Army Corps of Engineers, a federal government agency responsible for maintaining the quality and safety of America's waterways. Throughout this century the Corps has been instrumental in protecting lives, homes, and property through study and design of dams, levees, flood control systems, and other large-scale water projects.

Flash flooding due to levee breaks, dam failures, and other sudden events have unbelievable power: a wall of water can tear a poorly anchored home from its foundation and carry it away. (California Department of Water Resources)

layers change in consistency, there is a weak point in the levee. For this reason all levees should not be viewed as identical, and some prove far more reliable than others. The problem is that flaws are concealed and go undetected beneath the newest covering of soil until the levee first begins to show signs of failure.

Because levees are in flood plains, they tend to support a tremendous amount of vegetation. There is an ongoing effort to control vegetation on most systems because the roots of trees and some shrubs can cause irregularities in the compacted layers inside the levee. Secondly, vegetation provides cover for burrowing animals and rodents, which tunnel into the compacted soil of a levee and offer an inroad for flood waters to damage the levee core. In fact, during the early years of New Orleans, one of the major causes of levee damage was attributed to rooting hogs wandering the countryside. In some communities the levees are set on fire each year during the dry season in order to burn off grasses and weeds before inspections can begin. Older, poorly maintained levees may be choked with vegetation and thus are not very reliable.

There are a number of other ways a levee can fail. If it is built upon a sand-based soil rather than a dense clay, the ground beneath it can shift or completely disappear. The scouring effect of fast-moving water, particularly on bends of certain angles, can erode away the base soil beneath the levee if it is not strong enough to resist such action. Levees were often built or relocated to preserve valuable riverbank property, decisions which may have placed them

The size of this substantial levee can be compared to the two-lane road that was built on top. It has failed in two different places, which shows how unpredictable the stability of a levee can be when saturated with this much water pushing against it. There are the remnants of unsuccessful emergency repairs in two places, evidenced by piles of sandbags and areas protected by plastic sheeting. (California Department of Water Resources)

on sandy, unstable soils. In fact, history shows us that levee failures often recur in the same place due to an inherent flaw in the location or alignment of the levee, because of naturally unstable soil, or when the river channel is particularly unruly.

BOILS A boil is simply water seeping not through but *beneath* the levee to appear on the dry side. Boils can be seen frequently along flooded levees. A boil in itself is not particularly dangerous, but when it carries soil particles, it is relabeled a **sand boil**, which is *very* dangerous. Sometimes a boil is just a slow flow, barely noticeable, but in many historic cases they have been referred to as **spouts** due to the water pressure. A boil usually starts small, the movement of water beneath the levee insufficient to dislodge soil particles from the levee itself or from the base soil the levee sits upon. Eventually the soil becomes so saturated it begins to disintegrate, invisibly eroding away a cavity beneath the levee. When that is of sufficient size, the entire levee section simply collapses into the hole.

Water seeps beneath the levee because it follows the path of least resistance. Engineers understand that if they can create equal pressure on the dry side, there will be enough resistance to stop the flow. To do this they surround the boil on the dry side with a tightly built ring of sandbags, continuing to make it higher until the pressure is equal on both sides. When the water stops flowing, there is no longer the risk of more soil being carried out from beneath the levee. These rings of sandbags are commonly called **chimneys**; when a levee is heavily flooded and suffering boils, there may be dozens of them along its entire length.

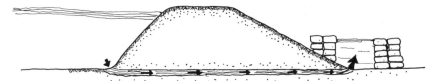

Diagram of a levee boil. The water on the flooded side seeks out a weak point at the toe of the levee and begins to work its way underneath. It then "daylights" on the dry side, boiling up out of the earth as if in a pan of hot water. In order to equalize the pressure, a chimney of sandbags is built around the boil. The height of the chimney must be increased until the downward gravitational pressure of the water sitting in the chimney equals that which is pushing up from under the levee.

SLIDES Slides or sloughing can be very serious and may hint at impending levee failure. Slides occur when the levee becomes so saturated that the soil on the dry side can no longer remain in place on a sloping incline. An early sign that a slide is likely to occur is horizontal cracking in the face of the levee. If a crack does appear, sandbagging or earth pushed up against the base of the levee supports the sagging section from underneath. There can be heavy equipment scraping the surrounding earth for hours and pushing layer after layer up against the levee. There can be a problem finding a sufficient amount of earth for such an effort in an urban area packed up tight against a levee. Trucks of fill may not come fast enough for the effort to be successful, as was the case many times over during the 1993 floods on the Mississippi.

Sometimes slides are caused by wave action or a strong current pushing on a portion of the levee, forcing water at a higher pressure than normal into the levee side. In this case, there is the need to place additional earth into the river to reduce the rate that water is seeping through. This earth must be further protected by loads of rock and gravel because it cannot be properly compacted. In addition, the rock provides a stronger barrier to the erosive forces of flood water and the additional concussions of floating debris ramming directly into the levee sides.

Crews must continually shore up levees that are disintegrating due to slides or wave action. (California Department of Water Resources)

OVERTOPPING In many instances during the summer of 1993, water levels exceeded the heights of the levees. This was in part due to the decrease in river capacity from a half-century of sedimentation. When many of the levees were built, the **runoff coefficients** (simply, the amounts of runoff) were less than they are today. Remember, less vegetation and more development mean increased runoff.

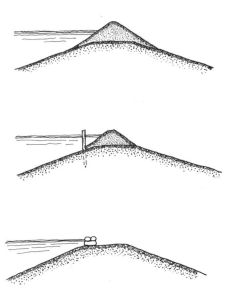

When water flows over a levee, the surface erosion rate is extreme because levee tops aren't designed, as are dams, to withstand this event. The levee can be worn down very quickly once it is first overtopped, a fact offering very little time for evacuation or repairs. Engineers have no choice but to raise the height of a levee *before* the water can overtop it, or lose their chance to save the levee at all. Once the levee is overtopped, there is no way to get equipment and fill material close enough to make repairs safely.

Three examples of ways levee heights are increased. When there is danger of overtopping, levees must be raised very quickly. This can be a nearly impossible task when large expanses of levees are involved. Engineers decide which method to use based on the availability of equipment, materials, and manpower. Top: Add fill dirt to the top of the levee. Center: Install a protective barrier of wood or steel panels which reduce the erosive wave action, with a backup of fill behind. Bottom: Raising a levee with sandbag walls.

There are a number of methods for raising levee heights in emergency situations. Walls of sandbags are time-consuming to build and require a tremendous labor force. Concrete barriers, steel sheeting, or simply more earth piled on top of the levee are frequent remedies. The biggest problem with earth fill is that an incredible amount is required to raise a levee just a few inches. When there is a race with time, this can be difficult if not impossible to accomplish even with heavy equipment.

Ponding is another type of flooding more common in coastal conditions, but it may also occur near lakes or dry ponds during wet years. You need not be in a valley or a low spot to experience flooding. In many situations, low-lying ground may simply **pond**, holding water until it gradually percolates into the soil. With no river or stream to carry the water away, the flooded pond area may become quite large, much like an inland lake with a radically fluctuating

Coastal flooding is some of the most serious because hurricanes coupled with high tides can cause long-term inundation. (California Department of Water Resources)

Aerial view of flooding that extends unchecked for miles on every side of this river. (California Department of Water Resources)

water level. Extreme rainfall during "unusual" years may cause water levels to rise and inundate surrounding residential areas.

IDENTIFICATION OF FLOOD-PRONE HOMESITES

One of the best ways to increase your chance of surviving a flood is to understand the vulnerability of your home or one you intend to purchase. The chief point to remember is that water always flows downhill. If a site is in a valley, the watershed that feeds that valley will generate a certain amount of runoff during a normal year. In most areas officials have calculated its volume based on vegetation, degree of slope, soil type, and, most importantly, rainfall records. A valley in a region with high rainfall is more likely to experience floods than one in an arid climate, although flash flooding is always a possibility.

It becomes more difficult to visualize a watershed when you are dealing with flat land, such as that of many midwestern and southern states. The degree of slope may be minimal, but the watershed can be massive, with flood plains extending miles beyond the limits of a river channel in practically every direction. With the Mississippi's watershed covering roughly 30%

Towns such as this have withstood periodic flooding for a long time, which can severely affect the economy and safety of residents. These are the communities that derive the greatest benefit from the National Flood Insurance Program. (California Department of Water Resources)

of the United States, it would be difficult to live within the watershed yet not live in some sort of a flood plain on either that great river or her many tributaries.

In the past, flood disasters have plagued many communities to the point that their entire economic bases were strained to the limit. Yet due to their strategic locations on rivers of commerce, these communities persisted despite the repeated floods that wrecked homes and lives. Some people moved away, but others knew no other hometown and chose to remain and deal with high water. This example of human nature shows needs most of us share: a home and the sort of permanence found only when many generations have shared the same familiar surroundings. This feeling doesn't apply just to flood-prone areas: It is equally strong in those who live on the Atlantic Coast and must contend with hurricanes, and those who love the Rocky Mountains despite avalanches and forest fires.

This flash flood event shows how residential areas that are not protected by levees suffer serious erosion. In this case a back yard swimming pool is separated from the river by a thin margin of embankment protected by sandbags, plastic, and wood shoring. (California Department of Water Resources)

The National Flood Insurance Program

It is for these flood-ravaged communities that the National Flood Insurance Program was created as a means of providing some compensation after flood events. There are many benefits to this program, one of which provides the means to accurately determine the threat of flooding on a particular homesite *before* you buy it. In many cases, knowing the degree of risk can be used as a bargaining chip, which places the buyer at a greater advantage.

Dry stream beds such as this in low-lying areas of the West can be subject to sudden flash flooding, which often takes people by surprise. (California Department of Water Resources)

In the past, private insurance companies were naturally reluctant to underwrite flood insurance on homes that had been repeatedly damaged by high water. If they did write such policies, the premiums were so high it was practically impossible for anyone but the very rich to afford

FLASH FLOODS

You probably don't think about flooding in the desert, but it occurs frequently in many of the arid western states, where sudden thunderstorms drop large amounts of water in a very short time. It also happens in other regions that experience summer cloudbursts. Warm tropical storms in winter can suddenly melt a large volume of ice and snow. Flash flooding can follow unexpected catastrophes, such as dam breaks. The rescue television programs are filled with motorists caught in flash flood waters, and most flood-related deaths are attributed to such circumstances. Flash flooding can follow just minutes or hours after a sudden cloudburst, but the flooding need not even be in the area experiencing the rainfall. Flash flooding is so deadly because people aren't ready for it.

Flash flooding should be of particular interest to anyone living close to dry washes, or arroyos, in the western states. They can fill and overflow their banks in moments, whisking away people, livestock, pets, structures, fencing, and even boulders. This is more serious when the event occurs at night, while residents are sleeping and unaware. These fast-moving waters are so powerful they push along vehicles, which act as battering rams against anything in their paths. The water has the force to change the topography of the land, scouring away soil, embankments, dams, and levees. It pays to stay tuned to weather broadcasts whenever there are thunderstorms in your area or in nearby highlands. In 1972, for example, 236 people died when a flash flood inundated Rapid City, South Dakota, after a thunderstorm in the Black Hills.

coverage. As flood-ravaged communities continued to grow, the cost of federal emergency aid and services became enormous and far out of proportion to the population base. Concerned that these communities were destined to remain in poverty due to unruly rivers, the federal government went to work on a plan to a) provide flood insurance at affordable rates to homeowners and b) provide an incentive for flood-prone communities to develop flood control systems.

In response to this need, Congress passed the National Flood Insurance Act of 1968, later modifying this original document with the Flood Disaster Protection Act in 1973. In short, this legislation provided the means of creating a single national flood insurance program for the whole country. This allowed the losses in one region or community to be spread out over a much

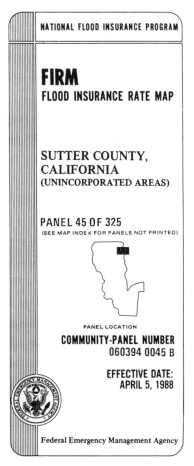

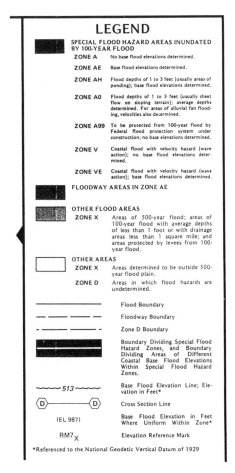

Flood Insurance Rate Maps. The FIRMs are organized into panels that fit over the designated coverage area. The cover shows where the map area is located. The sample legend shows the different zones that are used on the maps and how other information is depicted.

larger base, thus lowering the cost of premiums. The resulting National Flood Insurance Program (NFIP) involves a number of government agencies but is primarily implemented by the Federal Emergency Management Agency (FEMA), as well as local private insurance agents, who are in charge of writing the policies.

But the NFIP does not automatically become available to everyone in a flood-prone area. As mentioned above, certain requirements must first be met by the community before the program is applied. This begins with the willingness to make changes and become responsible for flood control mechanisms such as levees, floodwalls, and ditch systems, just to name a few. A community's specific requirements are determined by a study conducted by the Army Corps of Engineers. Problem areas are identified, and plans are made to modify them as much as possible. Some of these plans spread out changes over many decades; some call for immediate action.

Part of such a study involves mapping the community in detail, with elevations of land taken at regular intervals throughout the flood plain. These maps, called **Flood Insurance Rate Maps** (FIRM), are used to establish the cost rate for coverage of a home. A completed map accurately shows where a homesite lies in terms of floods at various intensities. Homes may fall into one of these basic categories:

Zone A series   Area of 100-year flood plain
Base flood elevation (BFE)
Special Flood Hazard Area

Zone B   Area between 100-year flood plain and 500-year flood
or Zone X   plain
Minimal Flood Hazard Area

Zone V   Coastal high hazard areas

Most flood damage occurs in the 100-year flood zone, which is why homes that lie inside this boundary are identified as Special Flood Hazard Area sites. The depth of flooding in this A zone varies, as indicated by spot elevations and A-series subcategories, such as A0 or A99. The base flood elevation, set at the 100-year flood boundary, dictates how problems such as floodproofing measures are to be handled. Serious flooding has also occurred in the B or X 500-year flood zone, which is classified as a considerably lower hazard zone.

≣≣

There is often confusion as to exactly what the "100-year flood" designation means. According to FEMA, this does not refer to a flood that occurs once every 100 years. It means a flood of that level has at least a 1% chance of being equaled or exceeded in any given year. It is interesting to note that the 1994 flooding in the southeastern states has been deemed a 500-year flood, or occurring in a "minimal flood area."

≣≣

There are many rules and regulations associated with participation in the NFIP, and flood control efforts should be ongoing. If deficiencies in community actions are identified by FEMA, there may be restrictions, probationary periods, and even penalties. The reason for such controls relates to the second purpose of the NFIP: to encourage the establishment of permanent flood control measures in the community.

The areas designated by FIRM will also experience certain controls and restrictions regarding future development. This is very important if you are considering a purchase of unimproved land or vacant lots within designated areas. The Department of Housing and Urban Development (HUD) has defined finish elevation clearances and building design regulations to ensure that dwellings in hazard areas are properly constructed, if allowed at all. There is fear that new structures within the 100-year flood zone will displace a proportionate volume of water, thus lowering the capacity of this zone. Objects of any size also alter the way water flows and may cause damage elsewhere or overtax what flood control measures have been constructed.

Often the requirements of HUD as well as lending institutions differ from those of local government agencies, a problem that can lead to difficulties when potential buyers are seeking a HUD-insured mortgage. To avoid such complications, when you consider buying a home in a flood-prone community, be aware of its status on the FIRM. If in doubt or you find the research too complex, hire a licensed land surveyor or civil engineer to locate the site on the

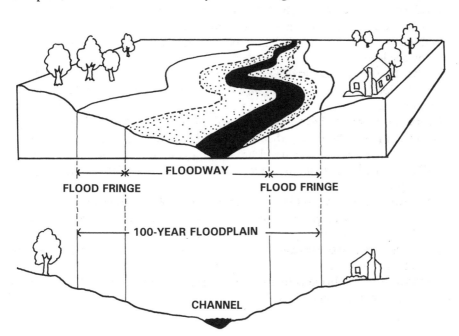

This diagram illustrates how a flood plain is broken down. The river channel is the normal flow line of the river. The floodway includes areas that may be inundated with flooding during normal high water of spring snowmelt or a typical rainy season. The 100-year flood plain extends even further, encompassing the channel, floodway, and the flood fringe on either side. Although it is not shown, the 500-year flood plain would extend even further beyond the flood fringe.

maps and provide you with a brief report as to its status in the flood plain. The small fee for these services can save you tens of thousands in flood damage.

For more information contact the nearest FEMA office. For a look at your community in terms of FIRM mapping, take a trip to the city hall and ask for the maps. They are free for public viewing, and FEMA will tell you how to obtain your own copy or a whole set if need be from the flood map distribution center. The professional resources and research that went into establishment of NFIP and delineation of the maps was done for your benefit, one of the best uses of public tax dollars.

The flood insurance program and the rate maps can be confusing to you at first, but water movement on the land and the unpredictability of our great rivers is equally confusing. The following are some basic definitions and abbreviations used in the program. There is a more detailed discussion of how you can obtain this type of flood insurance in chapter 7.

Flood Insurance Program Definitions

BASE FLOOD, 100-YEAR FLOOD The flood having a 1% probability of being equaled or exceeded in any given year.

BASE FLOOD ELEVATION (BFE) The height of the base flood in relation to other national data, typically sea level. For example, the elevation of a flood 1 foot deep may be labeled "EL. 123" because it is 123 feet above the reference point, sea level.

FLOOD INSURANCE STUDY (FIS) Engineering study performed by FEMA to identify flood-prone areas, insurance risk zones, and other flood data within a community.

FLOOD INSURANCE RATE MAP (FIRM) Insurance and flood plain management map issued by FEMA that identifies, based on detailed or approximate analyses, areas of 100-year flood hazard in a community. Also shown on the FIRM are actuarial insurance rate zones, BFEs, and 500-year flood plain boundaries.

NATIONAL FLOOD INSURANCE PROGRAM (NFIP) Federal program under which flood-prone areas are identified and flood insurance is made available to the owners of property in participating communities.

LACUSTRINE FLOOD HAZARD AREA Area subject to inundation by flooding from lakes and ponds.

RIVERINE FLOOD HAZARD AREA Area subject to inundation by flooding from streams, such as rivers and creeks.

2
UNDERSTANDING RIVERS, CREEKS, AND SEASONAL STREAMS

People "cannot tame that lawless stream, cannot curb it or con-
fine it, cannot say to it, Go here or go there, and make it obey."
Mark Twain
Life on the Mississippi

There are few amenities like moving water. It speaks to us, it is ever changing—streams are the lifeblood of the natural world. They have figured in
American literature as living things that become as strong a part of us as
do mountains and prairies.

Communities located near our nation's great rivers, such as the
Mississippi, the Ohio, the Colorado, and the Sacramento, are well aware of
both the benefits and the flood potential of bodies of water. But large rivers and
lakes are fed by thousands of smaller tributaries, helping to collect and carry
water draining from higher points of
land. These smaller drainages are
called creeks, streams, brooks,
rivers, and other local terms loosely
describing their size and character.

There are three aspects of streams
and rivers we must consider because
they are closely related. Most obvious are the ecosystems that border
streams, the communities of plants
and animals that gather where there
is suitable cover, food, and water.
Second is the threat to humans,
land, and property when these
drainages flood. Third is the desta-
bilization and erosion of their banks, which can greatly change the nature of
the waterways. If the protective vegetation along streams and rivers is
removed or degraded, there is a greater threat of erosion and flooding.

*A small river with natural vegetation covering
the banks.* (California Department of Water
Resources)

Therefore, care of these vital conduits is essential if we are to preserve their fragile beauty and also benefit from these natural mechanisms.

It must be said that exact definitions of many of these waterways can be difficult. Many were originally manmade ditches to carry runoff or irrigation water and may still function in this respect. But a good number of them have been abandoned and today better resemble natural sloughs, sluggish creeks, or swamps than anything else. There is plenty of confusion over this issue when it comes to preservation of habitat. In the next chapter we will look at how these areas are classified and at the regulations now in place that limit how they can be treated, even on private property. This has become a bone of contention among many. **It is important to know that new federal regulations now in effect may prevent you from disturbing even a handful of dirt without a permit, and any stabilization effort or improvement of natural or manmade waterways may be illegal.**

STREAMS AND COMMUNITIES

Streams and other drainages that exist in and around residential areas increase the risk of flooding. But as discussed in chapter 1, flood events may occur

Aerial photos show how towns and residential areas tend to cling to the edges of rivers within the natural flood plain. This leaves very little space for the river to rise without damaging homes and property. (California Department of Water Resources)

24

infrequently, and the ability of a stream to overflow its banks is often neglected or overlooked due to such infrequency.

During this century there has been a tendency to encroach on these rural, suburban, and even urban streams as land prices rise and waterfront properties are in great demand. Because major floods can be separated by decades of low flows, there is a tendency for each new generation to take the threat of flooding more casually than the last. New homes are built just a little closer to the water's edge, marinas and restaurants pop up, and the old high-water marks are gradually forgotten. Only communities participating in the NFIP remain fully aware of this threat, as their development regulations are based on the FIRM, which establish high-water elevations.

As the population of the United States continues to rise, there is a gradual spreading of residential areas farther and farther from the center of town. Some scientists have termed this the **urban-wildland interface**, which describes the direct contact of residential developments with wild ecosystems. Creeks and streams often cross or are adjacent to homes, farms, and ranches. Unless we know how to care for these waterways and avoid activities that degrade them, there is always the potential to cause harm through ignorance. Should a stream already be suffering, much can be done to improve conditions, and perhaps in the process we reduce threats of flooding as well.

RIPARIAN HABITAT

Although we tend to see a flood event simply as human disaster, high water is a natural occurrence that fits into the larger ecological picture. To view a stream in the proper context, it is important to understand its role not only as a water channel, but as a source of life. Streams and rivers are usually fed by rainfall or snow-melt in the surrounding watershed. They can also be drainages for lakes, springs, and seepages of varying sizes. Some flow all year around, but others do so only during the spring runoff or just after rainstorms.

Although water is not always flowing, there can be plenty of invis-

Long before levees were built, most American rivers were bordered by dense riparian vegetation which literally teemed with life during the dry seasons. Much of this has been lost to flood control projects and with them went the important natural benefits they provide to bank stabilization. (California Department of Water Resources)

ible moisture trapped beneath the soil. This soil moisture is what supports the cottonwoods and willows in what appear to be dry washes of the arid western states. This is also the case on the prairie, where even during the early years of

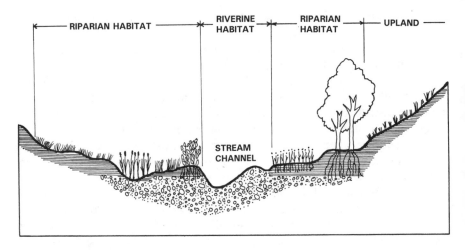

Cross Section of Riparian Stream Habitat
The vegetation of riparian areas varies as it transitions from the marshy stream channel to dry uplands.

settlement, the only source of wood might be from cottonwood trees growing along waterways. Farther to the west there was considerable vegetation along the river courses: dense thickets of willows, crowded groves of cottonwoods, wild grapevines, blackberry brambles, and wild roses. These plants sit upon a shelf that raises them above the main channel of a river or stream so that only when it is in flood state do they stand in water. The rest of the time, they constitute a forestlike ecosystem. Seen from the air during the dry months, these ribbons of green may be the only water and cover for miles, essential to wildlife.

Vegetation termed **riparian** is found on the banks of rivers and streams. Much of it was destroyed to create farmland, to build levees, and as fodder for livestock. Riparian areas are not technically wetlands, but they do share many functions with recognized wetland ecosystems. For example, riparian trees, shrubs, and vines filter runoff, slow the velocity of high water, and help hold stream banks against erosion.

Riparian ecosystems are well defined in arid climates due to marked differences from the surrounding prairie, desert, or dry scrub. Similar conditions can be seen in the eastern states and the South, where they usually connect with bottomland hardwood swamps, which cover far more area than the riparian strips. A riparian ecosystem may blend with marshy growth of reeds, grasses, and sedges as it drops down to the main channel of the stream. In fact, riparian vegetation acts as a buffer to protect the marshy ground and also keeps the stream channel well defined and static.

Species of animals and insects gather in riparian areas to feed off the abundant plant life, completing a food chain that relies upon the life-giving waters of a stream. Riparian areas are also important breeding grounds for many species. The abundant vegetation provides protective cover for ground-nesting birds. Thick stands of grasses are important grazing areas for deer and herbivores, particularly during dry seasons. Trees house birds and small mammals seeking protection in the canopy branches.

Vegetation within riparian areas can consist of trees, shrubs, vines, grasses, and perennials, all of which help to sustain the stream's viability and ensure consistent water quality. Riparian vegetation protects the stream, and the stream supports the vegetation in several ways:

1. Woody and herbaceous plants slow the speed of flood waters, thus reducing flood damage potential.
2. The foliage of larger plants helps shade the soil from the heat and drying effects of direct sunlight. This keeps plant roots cool and reduces evaporation from both soil and water surfaces.
3. A dense network of roots helps bind the banks of streams and keep them intact even when flows are increased.
4. Vegetation filters out sediment and pollution, which would collect in downstream lakes, reservoirs, flood control structures, and hydroelectric plants.

Think of riparian areas as giant filters. One of the greatest threats to water quality in our lakes is pollution in the runoff, which travels via freshwater rivers and streams. This is not just the pesticides, herbicides, and toxic by-products of industry we all recognize as hazards. Nutrients, which are actually food for plants, are equally dangerous, but in a different way. Two of the many sources of nutrients in runoff are lawns and agriculture, using chemical fertilizers, and nitrate-rich areas of intensive livestock use, where water drains through concentrations of manure.

Riparian vegetation is very important in mountain or hill country streams where steep grades increase flow rates of runoff, which causes rapid erosion.

As the nutrients build up in our waters, algae, which are tiny plants, thrive and multiply in the rich waters. This **nutrient loading** speeds up the natural process of eutrophication, which quickly degrades water quality. Riparian vegetation in the past gobbled up nutrients in runoff before they could enter a stream, but the increase of manmade nutrient sources combined with diminished riparian areas means the filtration mechanism cannot functioning properly. There is more on eutrophication in the next chapter.

Riparian areas represent some of the most threatened habitats in America because settlement and development are attracted to the beauty and resources of such areas. Our nation's rapidly growing population, particularly that of dry western states, is placing further demands upon these fragile natural areas. The difficulty is balancing the demands of our population with those of wildlife and habitat. There is no easy solution, but many government agencies are struggling with the problem, which is sure to remain controversial for decades to come.

≣≣

Tonto Creek was timbered with the local creek bottom type of timber from bluff to bluff, the water seeped rather than flowed down through a series of sloughs, and fish over a foot in length could be caught with little trouble. Today this same creek bottom is little more than a gravel bar from bluff to bluff. The old trees are gone. Some were cut for fuel, many others were cut for cattle during droughts and for winter feed, and many were washed away during the floods that rushed down the stream nearly every year since the range started to deplete. The same condition applies to practically every stream on the Tonto.

Fred Croxen, Senior Forest Ranger,
Tonto National Forest, 1926

≣≣

Western Riparian Areas and Ranching

Cattle and sheep have grazed the western states for well over a century. In some cases ranchers have set fire to large tracts of land to encourage a greater abundance of nutritious grasses. The federal government has historically leased grazing rights to individuals in order to generate revenue and put wildland ecosystems to work for food production. Grazing also occurs on private ranches large and small. This has many ecologists concerned for the quality of riparian vegetation and marshes in rivers and streams.

Domestic livestock gather in herds wherever there is water and grass in the dry season. They usually congregate in riparian areas for long periods of time, consuming the soil-holding bunch grasses and even browsing willows and other shrubby species until they are but leafless twigs. It's not difficult to see how overgrazing riparian areas can have a devastating effect on the benefits of riparian ecosystems. The results are vastly decreased wildlife densities, increased erosion and bank destabilization, and, even worse, a dropping of the

This range has been over-grazed and very little vegetation remains. Riparian vegetation as well as marshy plants are destroyed by irresponsible ranching practices, but this problem is improving as cattlemen realize that it is to their benefit that streams are preserved from livestock degradation. (California Department of Water Resources)

IMPORTANT THINGS YOU CAN DO TO AVOID DEGRADING HEALTHY RIPARIAN HABITATS

Few of us want to see our riparian habitats degraded, but practices we take for granted often contribute to the problem. As responsible stewards of the environment, it is important to understand the different ways that riparian areas are damaged in order to reduce problems whenever we can.

1. Domestic livestock, such as cattle and sheep, grazing in riparian habitats consume vital vegetation and compact the soil. As a result many streams have experienced severe bank erosion and degraded water quality.
   Do not allow your domestic animals direct access to streams.
2. Drainage from homes, farms, and industry causes erosion and pollution in riparian areas, which destroys many of their benefits.
   Drain homesites and livestock areas *away* from streambanks.
3. Dumping of backyard rubbish into streams has resulted in the introduction of pollutants and aggressive exotic plants, which crowd out the important native species and reduce the ability to support wildlife.
   Do not dump garbage, fill material, or backyard refuse in or near streams.
4. Clearing land, mass grading of soil, and other disturbances have caused increased runoff and siltation of riparian areas to such an extent that streams could change their courses.
   Avoid clearing or grading that has impact on nearby streams or drainages.

water levels. A stream degraded by overgrazing can actually disappear, as evaporation and other effects reduce the amount of water and how it is distributed in the channel. During drought or even a normal dry season in very arid country, this loss of water becomes an emergency for both livestock and wildlife dependent on just a few sources.

Trampling and soil compaction are two other problems often found along stream banks where domestic livestock have access. Imagine the weight of a mature steer concentrated onto four small hoofs; then consider the pounds per square inch of pressure upon damp soil. In many cases this is a clay soil, which is plastic in nature and easily molded when wet. Compacted soil does not readily support regrowth of new grass, and if the livestock remain it is virtually impossible for the stream to repair itself. This is why the Soil Conservation Service and other water quality agencies are so concerned about grazing and stream quality.

If there is a similar situation on your property, it can be repaired with a number of techniques provided by these agencies. Certain grazing strategies are known to have a positive effect on revitalization of degraded riparian and streamside ecosystems. Many successful projects have been completed on public and private land nationwide. Here are some of the practices that can be applied to our own farms, ranches, or country homes where streams are present:

1. Include the riparian area within a separate pasture.
2. Fence or herd livestock out of riparian areas for as long as necessary to allow vegetation to recover.
3. Control the timing of grazing to keep livestock off streambanks when they are most vulnerable to damage.
4. Add a longer rest cycle to grazing and limit the intensity (fewer animals).
5. Permanently exclude livestock from riparian areas that are overly sensitive and at high risk.

Recognizing the Signs of Healthy and Degraded Riparian Areas
The EPA has established some valuable guidelines to help you recognize a degraded riparian area and how it differs from a healthy stream ecosystem.

1. Healthy: **Diverse vegetation** and root systems protect and stabilize streambanks; stream shaded. Degraded: Little vegetation to protect and stabilize streambanks and shade stream.
2. Healthy: **Elevated water table** and saturated zone; increased subsurface water storage. Degraded: Lowered water table and saturated soil zone; reduced subsurface water storage.
3. Healthy: **Increased summer stream flow**. Degraded: Reduced or no summer stream flow in places it once ran year round.

Healthy bank: A similar river bank bearing riparian vegetation that will stabilize the soil even during periods of inundation. Wildlife is abundant and well protected. (California Department of Water Resources)

Degraded bank: This example of a severely degraded river bank that exhibits most of the problems associated with loss of riparian vegetation. There are no plants to hold the bank or to filter out sediment. The bank is rapidly eroding away as the water scours the exposed edge. There is no food or cover for wildlife. (California Department of Water Resources)

This bank shows how water has scoured out a depression that will eventually collapse. The soil is then carried away with the water to create a sediment deposit somewhere else. This kind of erosion afflicts many western rivers and streams. (California Department of Water Resources)

4. Healthy: **Cooler** water in summer, **reduced icing** in winter. Degraded: Warm water in summer and icing in winter.
5. Healthy: **Improved habitat** for fish, wildlife, and other aquatic organisms. Degraded: Poor habitat for fish, wildlife, and other aquatic organisms.
6. Healthy: **Livestock forage increased** in quantity and quality. Degraded: Reduced amount and quality of livestock forage.

STREAMBANK PRESERVATION AND WATER QUALITY

When water twists and turns its way through a stream channel, its force is pitted against the banks. Certain banks take the full impact of the water, just as some walls around a racetrack are built up where drivers are likely to spin out if they don't follow the curve properly. Water can attack streambanks just as brutally as a race car can hit that wall.

Under normal conditions the scrub willows, grasses, and riparian trees protect the higher banks that contain the main stream channel. In many cases, the water never comes near these banks except during periods of peak flows. In a flooded state, water is forced into the twigs and foliage of bank vegetation, reducing its velocity before reaching the bank earth. What water does make it through has less of an erosive effect, due to the network of roots that bind the soil together. The force of the water cannot easily scour away the earth or undermine it.

In degraded riparian habitats of streams, as well as manmade ditches and virtually anything that channels moving water, these same forces are at work much of the time. In a degraded stream, each year's high water wears away a good portion of the streambank, far more so than would be the case if vegetation were in place. The water scours a depression at the base of what sometimes are very steep cliffs; when the support material is lost, huge chunks of rock and earth collapse into the stream. This loose material is easily carried away in the stream flow, which means there will be more sediment downstream in ponds, reservoirs, lakes, and wetlands. This bank erosion not only causes widening of that channel, it can also cause the stream to change course in order to flow around a new pile of earth. This is exactly what is threatening streams throughout America, most often in arid states of the west.

≡≡

Before about 1880, the Gila River channel from Santa Cruz Junction to Yuma was narrow with firm banks bordered by cottonwoods and willows, but by the early 1890s it occupied a sandy waste from one-quarter to one-half mile wide."

J. J. Wagoner,
*History of the Cattle Industry in
Southern Arizona*

≡≡

A healthy perennial stream will have a main channel of water deep enough to remain cool in summer, resist freezing in winter, and usually flow year round. This depth ensures water quality by maintaining a swift but well contained flow. A great many western streams and rivers suffer from grazing as well as mining and their combined erosive and sedimentary effects. Over the years, bank collapses have sent more and more silt into channels, and today a good number of them have a very wide but shallow flow, which often dries up in summer, the moisture lost deep in the new sediment deposits. This presents a hardship for wildlife and even makes it difficult for cattle to find water in the dry season.

Sometimes it's difficult to see the difference between a manmade drainage way and a natural stream. In some cases, there is no difference. For example, an irrigation ditch dug by Pueblo Indians hundreds of years ago may have become integrated into a natural regional drainage pattern, thus taking on the characteristics and roles of a natural stream. For this reason it is illegal to modify any waterway, even if it runs through or borders your property, without permission from the government. In part, this is because attempts at improvements can often go awry if the landowner doesn't have the knowledge to see the complexities of the task. Plus, there are wildlife considerations influencing how certain measures can be implemented for the greatest benefit.

Bank Stabilization
There are a number of ways to restore the integrity of streambanks and banks along manmade ditches and canals. If you would like to improve riparian habitat on your own land, take advantage of the USDA Soil Conservation Service, the US Fish & Wildlife Service, and other state or federal agencies that are there to help you plan the project. You may be required to enter a permit process, which makes certain that your activities won't have any ill effects downstream. This also ensures that your time and money spent on stream restoration have the greatest all-around effect without any negative environmental impact. Many feel these regulations are an expensive burden and infringe on the private property owner's rights; in many cases, this is true. But streams and rivers are unique in that a single one may extend for miles, sometimes across many states. With so many people and regions involved in flood control, water quality, as well as the health and longevity of a river, it is better to err on the side of overregulation.

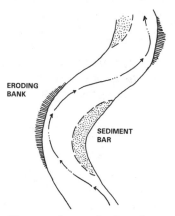

Diagram of stream bank erosion and sedimentation. Water erodes a bank on the outside of a curve, then deposits sediment on the inside bank.

Before you consider stabilizing a bank, it is important to see how hydrology influences the erosion process. The analogy of the racetrack shows how a stream **meanders**, or varies its alignment closer to some banks and further from others. The **flow line** of the main channel is usually the deepest point and has the strongest current. The flow line will meander through a sand and gravel **floodway** defined by earthen banks on either side, which establishes the main alignment for the stream. The banks act somewhat like levees to direct and confine the main channel. Therefore, if the banks curve, so must the channel and its flow line.

As shown in the diagram, a flow line running down the middle of the floodway encounters little resistance, but if the stream banks curve, the flow will encounter a bank, which forces it to veer off to one side. This encounter causes cutting away of the bank where water makes contact, which is then deflected, carrying the eroded soil to the opposite bank, where sand- and sediment bars develop. If you study rivers and streams, you'll notice how eroding banks and sandbars are distributed in a predictable pattern based on the curvature of the floodway.

≡≡≡

Revetment—A facing of stone or other material either permanently or temporarily placed along the edge of a stream, shoreline, or levee to stabilize the bank and protect it from the erosive action of water.

≡≡≡

Water channels suffer when there is too much bank erosion, as when due to lack of vegetative protection. Likewise, similar cutting effects can occur all along drainage swales and ditches, creating gullies that grow wider and wider. Controlling gullies is a problem virtually everywhere that concentrated flows of runoff erode away the soil. The solutions for streambank cutting and control of gully widening are very similar because both occur when there is a lack of soil-holding vegetation. The ideal long-term goal should be revegetation, but when serious erosion is occurring, it can be difficult to plant and support developing vegetation. This is why mechanical means are often the first measures employed to help support plants until they mature. These mechanical methods also act as armor to buffer the erosive force of fast-moving water and prevent any further soil loss.

RIPRAP If there is a good supply of rock available, riprap is a fine way of armoring banks and ditches that contain high-velocity flows after rainfall or snow-melt. This is simply rock cobble, which is not subject to much erosion and looks natural, lining a bank or an entire ditch. The irregular surface that results also slows down the velocity of the water and thus further reduces erosion. However, if there is a lot of sediment coming down from upstream, riprap is susceptible to being buried with silt. The size of riprap should increase with the velocity and volume of water flowing through the channel or gully.

Using riprap on your own homesite is a good idea to protect the edges of the raised pads used for floodproofing. You can grow plants in and around the cobbles to make them more attractive. You can otherwise apply mortar between the stones to better seal the surface and give the appearance of a stone wall.

When using riprap on a large scale, such as amending streambanks or lining ditches or gullies, it's important to consult an expert from the Soil Conservation Service (SCS). If the riprap were to wash away due to poor installation or cobbles too small to withstand the water velocity and volume, serious consequences could result downstream. This means of stabilization can be labor-intensive, and the cost to buy and transport cobble can be very high, due to its weight. An SCS agent will help you design and construct the project, as well as clarify any regulatory issues involved.

SACKED CONCRETE Sandbags have been widely used for over a century for protection of levees. Their flexibility and stability once placed makes them not only inexpensive but easy to make and use. They remain quite effective until the bag deteriorates. Sandbags filled with wet concrete rather than sand act much the same way but are longer lasting. A wall made of concrete-filled sacks will soon set up into quite a durable structure. When the bags disintegrate, the hardened concrete remains formed and in place indefinitely. All it lacks is steel reinforcement to provide the structural integrity of concrete blocks or poured concrete.

Sacked concrete has been used by many state highway departments in protecting the slopes around highway overpasses. The sacks aren't stacked into a vertical wall but in offset tiers, so that each row appears like a very wide step. Sacked concrete makes a good alternative to riprap where cobble is unavailable or too expensive. It also lends itself to irregularly shaped embankments or as culvert headwalls on difficult terrain, as it requires no forms.

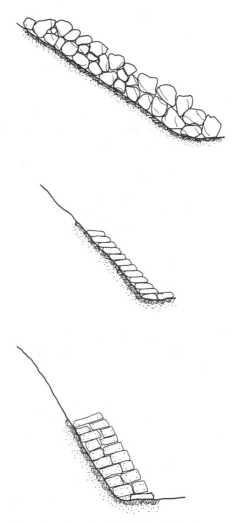

Examples of mechanical bank stabilization and revetment using three methods. Top: rock cobble riprap. Center: sacked concrete. Bottom: stacked concrete fragments.

Use this method to help reduce erosion on the edges of planting mounds and raised pads common to floodproofed homesites. Dry concrete/aggregate mix can be purchased at most home improvement stores and is easily mixed in a wheelbarrow and bagged. The wet sacks can be arranged with gaps to provide pockets for plants. You can also mix an earth-colored tint into the concrete for a more natural appearance after the bags decompose.

≡≡≡≡≡≡≡≡≡≡≡≡≡≡≡≡≡≡≡≡≡≡≡≡≡≡≡≡≡≡≡≡≡≡≡

When you are using riprap or sacked concrete, weeds eventually spring up in between. If ornamental or erosion-control plants are a part of the plan, weed control becomes a big maintenance chore. One solution is to grout in the spaces with wet concrete, but this isn't very attractive. The best short-term solution is to lay out and anchor weed-blocking fabric before you set the cobble or sacks. When you are ready to plant, cut a small hole in the fabric, set the plant, then smooth the fabric back down. This fabric will effectively block weeds until the desired plants mature. It is far better than plastic sheeting, which disintegrates from exposure to weather and sunlight. The fabric is woven and thus stays together, allowing exchange of air and filtration of water down to the plant roots while preventing new seedlings from sprouting.

≡≡≡≡≡≡≡≡≡≡≡≡≡≡≡≡≡≡≡≡≡≡≡≡≡≡≡≡≡≡≡≡≡≡≡

BRUSH, LIVING AND DEAD Early flood engineering manuals discussed the use of brush for revetment and erosion control. Dead brush acts as a wave buffer; as long as it can be stabilized, it remains effective. One method used large, tightly bound bundles of straight cuttings from 2 to 10 feet long, staked into levees or shorelines to keep in place. Bundles could also be lined up and tightly packed, then held down with wire fencing anchored along the corners and edges. Before modern heavy equipment, it was a slow and arduous process to transport and place rock during emergencies, but bundled brush was lightweight and far easier to handle. It served the purpose during a flood and decomposed afterward. If we consider dead brush for residential purposes, it is quite attractive though somewhat temporary.

Revetment made of willow wattling is ideal because it is both a mechanical stabilization device and a means of revegetating at the same time. This bundle of living willow is held together with bailing wire. It is half planted in a shallow trench dug into the slope and staked into place. The second stake below the bundle helps to support the weight of the bundle on the downhill portion of the trench. Once the wattling roots, there is no longer any need for support.

Living brush, commonly called **wattling**, provides more long-term effects. Wattling consists of bundles of 1-inch diameter willow whips, which can vary in length depending on the available material. The whips should be cut in fall or spring, and bundled with ties made of baling wire. Bundles can be anchored on the sides of gullies or as revetment on banks. If laid out perpendicular to the slope and anchored, they will help trap sediment. This is an excellent solution because not only does the wattle protect banks, but it **will take root and grow**, particularly if set in place before the sap begins to rise. This controls erosion and at the same time revegetates with native willow stock taken from nearby sources.

WIRE FENCES AND MATTRESSES Virtually any material that won't dissolve can be used for bank stabilization, but the problem is keeping it in place when there is a high flow. Woven wire is surprisingly strong if properly anchored and makes a good covering for other materials. The wire is either erected as a fence for revetments or laid out on the ground as a **mattress**. The wire itself provides no protection; it is simply a stabilizing mechanism for other materials. Highway engineers use wire revetment and mattresses to hold rock, sacked concrete, wattling, and brush.

This example of a culvert and a surrounding headwall is built of poured concrete with short sidewalls to channel the water and prevent undercutting of the pipe. (California Department of Water Resources)

Fence revetments are located at the toe of the slope, and the posts must be very well anchored. They are similar to the fences built along highways at the base of large, unstable slopes to catch any rocks before they can tumble down into the traffic lanes. Wire revetment *fences* can have stones or brush tightly packed behind them, which is an important method of stabilization where there is very little space for larger materials. Wire *mattresses* are used on gradual slopes that are subjected to sheet flows down their surfaces. The mattresses are simply pegged down on top of stone, brush, or wattling and may remain in place permanently. A wire mattress combined with wattling creates a formidable barrier quite similar to natural riparian vegetation in a very short time. Plus, it requires no alteration of the waterway, such as digging postholes, and thus creates little disturbance overall.

Culverts and Headwalls
Whenever a road, driveway, or footpath crosses a stream, a bridge or a culvert must be placed. A culvert is that familiar corrugated pipe you see running under roads to carry runoff. Culverts are essential to eliminating roadway washout during periods of high water, and selection of the proper size is based on the expected storm flows. If the culvert is too small, the water simply goes both

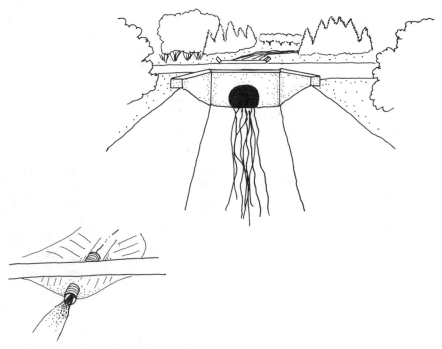

A culvert passing beneath a roadway or driveway must have a headwall to keep it in place. Culverts should always pass straight under the road (not at angles), which will force the water into one side wall or the other, but directly into the pipe.

through and over the top and thus has little effect, so it is better to use oversized culverts or discuss it with a civil engineer familiar with the area and its rainfall. A culvert should always be placed so that it runs perpendicular under the road.

Any channel twists and turns near the culvert entrance will cause the soil on either side to be scoured away and the culvert to become weak. A culvert must have a revetment or a **headwall** around the entrance if it is to remain in place. Without a headwall the water will undermine the culvert and cause it to float away; it can even be stood straight up on end. A headwall should have two **sidewalls** that stick out at angles to funnel the water into the culvert better, which is why, if you stop to notice, most culverts share the same design characteristics, no matter what the construction material.

Headwalls can be constructed out of cobble, poured concrete, concrete block, sacked concrete, or post and timber. The key is to seal the connection between the wall and the culvert because water is a tenacious finder of weakness. It's also a good idea to create a slight curb at the top so the road does not erode or drain down upon the culvert opening. Always remember to use culverts, even on footpaths, because without them you may start an uncontrolled gully where there was once just a tiny seasonal drainage.

3
WASTELANDS TO WETLANDS

Land drainage has been one of the principal factors in increasing the wealth and security of nations. Without the large areas of lands which drainage have made productive, it would not be possible to feed the present population of the earth.

During the past 75 years in the United States, over 53,000,000 acres of land have been rendered more productive by drainage. A large part of this area was practically worthless in its original state.

> George W. Pickels, Civil
> Engineer,
> *Drainage and Flood-Control
> Engineering*, 1925

A new image of these habitats has emerged. These areas have finally been recognized as a vital part of our landscape. Many are directly related to one of our most basic needs—water. Wetlands mitigate flooding, provide habitats for waterfowl, filter pollutants, and stabilize the biosphere, upon which all life is dependent. A new wetland ethic now advocates the protection and preservation of these areas.

> William A. Niering,
> *The Audubon Society Nature
> Guides: Wetlands*, 1985

Any piece of land that was soggy and subjected to periodic flooding was considered wasteland in the past. George Pickels represents the early twentieth-century attitude toward land management, with flood control and agriculture the primary goals. Land was valued only if it produced crops of one sort or another, and wet ground was incapable of supporting most food plants.

In contrast, William Niering's comment 60 years later illustrates the dramatic change in our view of these waste places, as we all have come to understand more fully how water, plants, and animals are inextricably linked in nature. The realization that these low-lying wetlands are also beneficial for more reliable flood control, as a strainer to reduce sediment in rivers, and as pollution filters would appeal to Pickels if he were in practice today.

Exactly what is a **wetland**? According to the EPA, "wetlands are those areas that are inundated or saturated by surface or ground water at a frequency and duration sufficient to support, and that under normal circumstances do support, a prevalence of vegetation typically adapted for life in saturated soil conditions. Wetlands generally include swamps, marshes, bogs, and similar areas."

An alpine meadow fed by a stream during the dry season. (California Department of Water Resources)

Today a new movement is afoot to preserve wetlands because they support a diversity of plant and animal life important to the environmental quality of our country. A vast number of species require the rich wetland habitat to reproduce, and we cannot successfully encourage wildlife if these areas are lost. Collectively called wetlands, there are many different types of waterways falling under this EPA definition, from riverbanks to swamps and prairie potholes. There are some that occur only in specific regions, some that are wet for only a short time each year, some manmade, and others purely natural. These waterways can be landlocked and still or flow all the way to the sea.

The majority of wetlands are of fresh water, with only about 5% located in coastal estuaries. Sometimes there can be difficulty separating coastal salt water wetlands from those of fresh water slightly inland, particularly in places such as the Florida coast, with its myriad waterways.

The government agencies charged with preservation of wetlands have set forth three basic qualities that indicate whether or not a wetland exists. If a site exhibits all three factors, then it is officially deemed a wetland and subject to a number of regulations to guarantee its survival.

1. **Hydric Soil** When soil is saturated with water during the growing season, soil organisms consume all the oxygen, which limits the type of veg-

Low river valleys were once part of vast wetlands that provided habitat for all sorts of wildlife. Here they were drained and turned to agriculture—typical scenario all across North America. Rising waters of this river never greet the surrounding flood plain, significantly reducing the great wetlands that supported flocks of migrating waterfowl. (California Department of Water Resources)

etation that can grow there. Under these conditions the soil becomes hydric, its main characteristic being a thick layer of decomposing plant material on the surface. Deeper down it is bluish gray, gray, or sometimes black. It emits an odor of rotten eggs.

2. **Vegetation** Only certain species of plants are capable of growing in hydric soil. Technically termed **hydrophytes**, they indicate a wetland condition in the area where they are growing. Around the edges of hydric soil, there are borderline plants that can tolerate some hydric conditions or thrive in the moist soil. The presence of these **indicator plants** helps define the site as a wetland. The US Fish and Wildlife Service has published lists of indicator plant species in order to assist field personnel in proper identification. Typical hydrophytes include cattails, bulrushes, cordgrass, bald cypress, willows, mangroves, and sedges.

3. **Hydrology** This term describes the presence and nature of water at the site, which during the dry season may not be readily apparent and thus a less reliable means of recognizing a wetland. The most important indicator is standing or flowing water during the growing season, indicative of perennial wetlands common in regions of heavy summer rainfall. Seasonal wetlands may dry out for a time, such as vernal pools and

An aerial view of large-scale land drainage efforts in the Sacramento River Delta, a vast network of sloughs, streams, and lagoons. Originally drained for agriculture in the early twentieth century, many of the resulting islands have been abandoned to revert to their original wetland status. (California Department of Water Resources)

prairie potholes. The amount of water, its depth, the seasons of inundation, and other hydrological facts are important to establishing that the wetland exists and classifying it. Other clues include high-water marks on trees, debris lodged against trunks or in shrubs, and sediment deposits, which also indicate water activity.

Wetlands can no longer be considered separately from issues of flood control. Before modern flood control, wetlands acted as holding tanks for high water. Before the levees were in place, rivers would swell and overflow their banks, with the excess water gathering in great pools wherever there were slight depressions in the land. This water remained "on hold" until the flood event passed and flow rates returned to normal in the river channels. The reserve water would later flow out of these holding ponds to drain gradually into the river. This process ensured that there was a constant supply of water in most rivers and streams throughout the dry season, which supported entire ecosystems.

With the advent of levees and large-scale land drainage projects, the water was prevented from gathering into the lowlands. A flooded river could no longer overflow, so *all* the water was forced to remain in the river channel

River deltas everywhere were drained to make the rich sediment deposits productive, but, as a result, the elevation of the land has subsided to well below the original elevation. These sites are now such a problem and so vulnerable to flooding that they are being abandoned and conservation groups such as Ducks Unlimited are working to return them to ideal nesting habitats. (California Department of Water Resources)

during the flood event. The lowlands themselves were either drained or filled in order to make them more agriculturally productive. Over the last century, development has increased all along our rivers, which has reduced soil absorption and generated even more runoff from surrounding watersheds. Even if there were no catastrophic storms, eventually this increase in flows would force levees higher and higher in order to contain the growing volume of runoff. Combine this with an occasional heavy-rainfall year, and you get the perfect recipe for deeper, faster, and bigger floods, as we have seen in 1993 and 1994.

There are other benefits to the holding tank concept of wetland flood control. While the water sits in the lowlands it is gradually percolating down through the soil to replenish the **water table**, which in most cases consists of gravel strata that can contain a large amount of water, called an **aquifer**. Groundwater supplies in many parts of the United States are declining because the aquifers are not being replenished as quickly as domestic wells are emptying them.

When an aquifer dries up, the spaces in the gravel once filled with water can collapse, causing ground subsidence. **Subsidence** is defined as a downward movement of the level of the ground surface caused by reduction of fluid pressure or organic matter volume within the soil. One profound example is in the San Joaquin Valley of California, where groundwater pumping for irrigation caused the land surface to drop by 29.6 feet from the 1920s to 1980. In fact, many believe this is one of the greatest manmade alterations in the configuration of the Earth's surface. Other obvious examples are the Florida sinkholes, which collapse without warning as underground water levels drop. The loss of wetlands has reduced the process of replenishment, so these underground water reserves are being used up faster than they are recharging. Only by recreating the original holding tank method of flood control can we be assured that this precious water resource will be preserved.

Another example of subsidence can be found in many river deltas. Deltas were first "reclaimed" for farming by draining this organically rich ground and surrounding it with levees to keep them from being flooded by seasonal high water. But gradually the soil dried out deeper down, so that oxygen began to infiltrate to lower levels. With the oxygen came rapid decomposition of centuries of built-up organic matter, consumed by microorganisms. What mineral soil remained had a much smaller volume. As a result, these islands have experienced a great deal of subsidence. For example, the elevations of some delta islands are today well over 5 feet below their levels prior to drainage, and they are still sinking. This places even greater burdens on the levees: While the islands were originally slightly higher than the surrounding river, now they would be entirely underwater if the levees were abandoned.

Development in low-lying wetlands causes still other problems. Often the water table remains just below the surface, although the earth appears drained and dried on top. A good example of this is in southern Louisiana, where all the graveyard crypts are aboveground because the water tables are too high. This water table is often the only source of drinking water for these communities. Any toxic materials or wastes introduced into the soil will seep down rather quickly into groundwater, helped along by rain or irrigation water percolating through the soil. While wetlands can act as pollution filters of surface water, deeper groundwater has no mechanism for cleansing itself once contaminated.

The US Army Corps of Engineers is rethinking some midwestern levee systems, with debate as to whether or not to rebuild some of them. The federal government is acquiring tracts of privately owned farmland in critical drainage areas in order to return the flood control system to its original reliance on wetlands. The additional benefits of wetlands, such as wildlife habitat and recreation, make a far more attractive alternative to rebuilding and long-term maintenance of levee systems.

Wetland regulations also control land use on both public and private land. The goal is to eliminate any alteration of wetlands to make them more suitable for development and agriculture. This is a benefit to us all because freshwater wetlands provide recreational uses, support various industries, and even influence coastal conditions. Many believe we have a sufficient amount of farmland, perhaps too much in the global scheme of things, and can easily sacrifice it to wildlife. And of course, there will always be resistance to development because many see builders as recipients of windfall profits. What is overlooked, though, is the long process of obtaining permits, payment of taxes and fees, and most of all the financial risks builders must endure on speculative ventures.

Life in flood-prone communities today is changing, and not everyone is pleased with this new direction. Many feel the restrictions on private land use are not fair to locals because a piece of land deemed an official wetland becomes undevelopable and loses its speculative value. Under a rigorous permit process monitored by the Army Corps of Engineers, some development may be allowed, but the mitigation demands, as well as the controls on what can occur under the permit, are subject to great controversy. Mitigation may involve creation of a new wetland or restoration of one that is currently degraded, both very expensive propositions. Unfortunately, the process of achieving such goals is not yet widely successful, with far more failures than is commonly known. Studies of recent projects illustrate the numerous ways a project can fail, a factor that becomes a bone of contention among those forced to pay for such potentially futile efforts.

HOW WE CLASSIFY WETLANDS AND THE WILDLIFE THEY SUPPORT

Simply stated, **wetlands** are the transitional areas between open water and dry land. Most wetlands are freshwater systems, with only 5% being coastal marine habitats. Since the 1700s the United States has lost over 53% of its wetland habitats, primarily due to drainage, dredging, filling, dams and levees, cultivation, grazing, pollution, mining spoils, and changes in both surface and underground hydrology. One fact that makes this issue so important is that 75% of our breeding bird population reproduces in wetlands. Much of our fishing industry relies on species that require coastal wetlands to spawn, hatch, and mature before returning to the sea. In fact, wetlands generate food and habitat for thousands of kinds of birds, fish, mammals, and insects.

With these areas playing such a critical role in the survival of North American wildlife, we now know that wildlife conservation efforts cannot be successful without taking into consideration wetlands and their relationships to various species. As a result, the federal government has charged four agencies with preservation of wetlands to ensure that there is "no net loss," as dictated by President Bush. They are the Environmental Protection Agency, the United States Army Corps of Engineers, the United States Department of Agriculture Soil Conservation Service, and the United States Fish and Wildlife Service. Refer to chapter 10 for information on how to contact these and other agencies related to wetlands and wildlife.

Only a small area of open water remains in this wetland as it becomes more shallow and supports hydric plant species. (California Department of Water Resources)

Here and there is revealed what is left of the pond. Now it resembles a wet meadow and will continue to become drier over time. (California Department of Water Resources)

A newly forming wetland marsh. (California Department of Water Resources)

Beaver activity creates dams, which cause smaller streams to back up and spread out into ponds. These are vital wetland habitats that are reappearing with the beaver, which were decimated during the nineteenth century. (California Department of Water Resources)

Ecological Succession

The ecological term **succession** is loosely defined as the slow, orderly progression of changes in vegetation in any area from the initial colonization to the climax. What this means is that virtually every ecosystem is in a continual state of change, which occurs slowly over hundreds or even thousands of years. There are certain plants called **climax species**, which indicate an ecosystem has reached the final, mature stages in succession. Among the most obvious examples

The edge of a lake with aquatic reeds growing in the shallows. (California Department of Water Resources)

are the old-growth redwood forests of the Pacific Coast. These trees have matured, shading out most of the plants beneath them so there are rarely any new plants growing under their canopies. Very little change occurs in these climax forests unless some sort of catastrophic event forces a change.

Evidence shows that most of our forests *have* experienced catastrophic changes, such as fires or the decimation in the wake of the Mount St. Helens eruption. These events destroy some or all of the climax species, which opens up the land again so that **colonizing species** are able to sprout and grow. These first colonizing plants, well known to inhabit newly disturbed ground, are usually grasses and perennials. Following colonization, **shrubs** represent the next group of plants to vegetate the site; they eventually crowd out the colonizers. Then trees begin to grow in the shade of the shrubs and fight their way through to eventually tower over the brush and thus shade them out of existence. These trees later become the **climax species**, dominating the forest until they are killed by either age, disease, overcrowding, wildfires, or when man is involved, as with logging.

Wetlands experience a similar process of succession, which began at the end of the last ice age after glaciers had pitted and scarred much of North America. Over 10,000 years ago, glacial runoff created rivers and streams, which flowed into the lowlands, which filled to become lakes. Succession here or in any lake begins with the sediment and other debris picked up by the flowing water and deposited into the lake, where it settles to the bottom. Over a very long period, the lake becomes more and more shallow. When the lake bed rises enough to allow sunlight to strike the bottom with sufficient intensity, plants adapted to water, such as algae, reeds, and grasses, begin to grow. These colonizers tend to appear first around the edge of lakes, where the water is more shallow than in the center. These plants in turn shed organic matter, which adds to the sediment, making the deeper portions in the center of the lake even more shallow. The plants gradually spread out and finally colonize the entire lakebed, at which point it has been transformed into a wetland **marsh**.

But succession does not stop here. The water level grows more shallow yet from the increased organic matter and at some point could be called a **wet meadow** or **prairie**. Becoming dry enough, the land supports woody shrubs, the vegetation change that marks a marsh's evolution into a **swamp**. The land mass continues to rise still higher, and this provides a suitable environment for trees, which generate a tremendous amount of litter. Soon the swamp rises and dries out completely, being reclassified as a **forest** of climax species.

Botanists and biologists have classified American wetlands into dozens of specific plant communities, depending on water level, soil, climate, and wildlife. Most loosely fall somewhere in the succession process between marsh and climax forest. In fact, some wetlands exhibit characteristics of all three at once, in a mosaic of different stages within a larger region. This mixed wetland can be the most beautiful and support the greatest diversity of wildlife. The best example of this is the Everglades, with its vast network of forests, shrub-choked swamps, and grassy wet prairies.

Following are some of the officially recognized wetland types.

FRESHWATER MARSHES You'll find these in every state wherever there is shallow standing water near lakes and rivers. Vegetation is predominantly grasses and grasslike plants, which provide breeding cover for amphibians, fish, and a wide assortment of insects.

SWAMPS These support dense stands of trees and shrubs. In some regions they are termed **bottomlands**, and they can be quite dry for parts of the year and partially wooded. They support an incredible array of birds, alligators, fur-bearing mammals, snakes, turtles, and the infamous hordes of insects breeding there in the humid summer months.

BOGS You'll find these in the cold far north, vegetated with plants adapted to acidic soils, such as sphagnum mosses, heathers, and some coniferous trees. Dead plant material does not decompose in bogs as it does in warmer climates, so the peat accumulates to great depths and often breaks away into floating islands. Birds, insects, reptiles, amphibians, rodents, beavers, and other mammals can be found living in bog wetlands.

PRAIRIE POTHOLES Most common in the northern Great Plains states, potholes are glacial depressions in the landscape that range from just a few feet across to well over a square mile. Water collects here, soils become hydric, vegetation abounds, and waterfowl gather in great numbers to breed and nest. During this century, farmers traditionally filled in great numbers of these wetlands to increase the amount of land in cultivation. This fact is now attributed as responsible for the decreased populations of ducks, geese, and other migratory water birds, most of which winter in the warm southern states, then migrate northward for the summer to breed in potholes and other wetlands.

WETLAND WILDLIFE HABITAT

As wetland preservation becomes more widespread and the habitats protected, we will come into greater contact with the wildlife they support. These creatures are firsthand examples of the earth's myriad species and their interdependence with plant life.

There are many people who fail to see the importance of these relationships because wetlands have been considered a nuisance or a real threat to human habitation. Perhaps the greatest fear is of mosquitoes, which are a

≡≡≡≡≡≡≡≡≡≡≡≡≡≡≡≡≡≡≡≡≡≡≡≡≡≡≡≡≡≡≡≡≡≡≡≡

Wetlands provide three important needs of wildlife:
food, water, and cover for nesting and shelter.

≡≡≡≡≡≡≡≡≡≡≡≡≡≡≡≡≡≡≡≡≡≡≡≡≡≡≡≡≡≡≡≡≡≡≡≡

serious problem in many regions where wetlands are plentiful. Malaria is the scourge of some climates, where only the *Anopheles* mosquito transmits the dreaded disease. Hundreds of thousands of people die of malaria each year worldwide. Another virus carried by mosquitoes is encephalitis, which is currently on the rise and is potentially deadly to both humans and animals. The fear of these two diseases by livestock ranchers and other residents has promoted widespread mosquito abatement efforts wherever there are wetlands supporting the mosquito life cycle.

Mosquitoes require standing water to reproduce, and in most wetlands there is plenty of it. However, mosquitoes are a part of the food chain, and a number of fish and other organisms feed on them and their larva. To control the hordes rising out of swamps and marshes at dusk, *Gambusia affinis*, a minnow commonly called the mosquitofish, has been introduced to

Mallards and other species of waterfowl are dependent on wetlands for food and nesting sites. They are the chief reason why hunting groups are so avidly supporting wetlands restoration, and though they do take birds in season, the increased population far outnumbers those lost each year. (California Department of Water Resources)

some areas to control mosquito populations without chemical sprays. Still, chemical controls are widespread in abatement districts where rice farming or wetlands are prolific breeding sites. This illustrates why there can be tremendous controversy over the presence, restoration, recreation, and protection of wetlands near developed areas.

It is important that anyone living in and around wetlands be aware of their fragile nature. Many wetlands mitigation projects are created very close to or within residential areas. These open spaces are different from public parks, yet few people realize this. A wetland cannot be managed as easily as a city park. The vegetation and any products of succession must be allowed to occur if the habitat is to support a wide variety of organisms.

It is not yet resolved how the presence of wetlands will affect nearby residents. There is much discussion on whether to require wetlands to be preserved as islands within developed areas, and some projects already in place may prove to be test sites. Perhaps the biggest problem with this is that residential areas house families, which usually include children, who find any natural open space wonderful to play in. It is understandable how their curiosity can disturb wildlife, such as ground-nesting birds, small fish, frogs, and turtles, and generally degrade the habitat. With the great effort and expense of preserving these wild pockets, it is the long-term human contact that may ultimately spell their demise.

Western Pond Turtle. Amphibians and reptiles are beneficial to wetlands. (California Department of Water Resources)

Wetlands and riparian habitat preservation are both directly linked to the population of salmon that spawn in headwater streams. There is controversy over many flood control and hydroelectric dams in rivers that inhibit the ability of fish to reach spawning grounds. Many believe that protection of wetlands will provide the regulatory power needed to ensure their survival. (California Department of Water Resources)

The ideal wetland conditions occur in large, protected areas designated wildlife preserves and in national or state parks. These may be considered land banks to be enlarged by purchasing land around their perimeters as compensation for smaller wetlands lost close to urban or suburban communities. Many feel land bank mitigation is a better use of our environmental resources, but others believe land banks are too few and far between to successfully increase wildlife habitat where it is most needed.

Water Weeds

One of the most difficult problems facing American wetlands today is invasive water weeds. These aquatic plants don't naturally occur in wetland habitats, yet once established are virtually impossible to eradicate. Wildlife experts as well as civil engineers both fear them for the same reasons.

One of the worst is hydrilla, an aquatic plant not native to North America that was first discovered growing wild in Florida in 1960. Hydrilla grows rapidly, putting on as much as an inch per day. If a plant is broken up, a new plant will sprout almost immediately from even the smallest fragment. Though they can't be sure, experts believe that the hydrilla was first introduced into American wetland waterways by aquarium dumping. In the very warm southern states and on the Pacific Coast, hydrilla has found an ideal home; in a very short time, it has literally invaded huge wetland areas and choked navigable waterways. In addition, the weed is affecting flood control, irrigation, and recreation.

Hydrilla

Hydrilla develops massive colonies that literally force out all other native aquatic plants essential to wildlife. With the competition falling by the wayside, there is nothing to check the hydrilla's growth. It will grow until the waterway is so packed with vegetation and the oxygen is so depleted that it kills most of the remaining life forms in the water.

You'll know hydrilla from other aquatic weeds by the following characteristics:

1. Rough-textured leaves with sawtooth edges. It feels rough when pulled through your hand.
2. Small spines on the underside of the leaf on the center vein.
3. Small potato-like, peanut-sized tubers on the roots.

When exotic plants move into our waterways they can take over. This example shows how water lilies have literally covered the entire surface of the water causing a disturbance in the natural wildlife balance and water quality.

In order to salvage an affected site, radical eradication measures are required. State agriculture or federal agencies should be notified of the problem; they will assess the (California Department of Water Resources)

SOME BIG PROBLEMS WITH WETLANDS IN DEVELOPED AREAS

Although there is a widespread love of nature and America's wild lands, when they are located too close to residential areas, a number of problems inevitably arise. Some are simply due to perceptions by individuals who retain preconceived notions of the value of the wild. For example, an older man who spent his life struggling to grow crops in his soggy fields may offer very little support for the protection of wetlands. He is likely to view them strictly as problem ground that should be drained to eliminate the mosquitoes and render it more productive.

There are a number of other issues that are legitimate concerns, as human nature is fairly predictable.

DUMPING GROUNDS With landfill costs rising, there will always be people who prefer to haul their garbage to a wooded wetland area and dump it under the cover of darkness than to pay a fee. Toxic wastes such as paint, gasoline, motor oil, and other chemicals are also dumped in these areas because landfills are very finicky about accepting them. This is also the case if no landfill is conveniently close. As careless as this seems, it is a reality that happens all the time.

PLANT POLLUTION If that lazy garbage dumper has some bamboo roots, honeysuckle berries, or, God forbid, some kudzu vine roots or prunings, the wetland can be seriously threatened. These and many other exotic plants are so well adapted they will smother the entire wetland, degrading habitat by denying cover and food plants essential to wildlife. Once established, they can be *extremely difficult* to eradicate! See the plant lists in chapter 9 for the worst offenders.

PET PROBLEMS Domestic cats and dogs wreak havoc with wildland ecosystems, particularly when they are strays. Dogs do chase away wildlife, but because they are usually well fed, the tendency to hunt, kill, and eat is not common. However, bird dogs and their kin are notorious for rooting out ground-nesting birds just for the fun of it.

By far the biggest threat to wetlands is domestic cats. People have a big problem with taking an unwanted feline to the pound, where it may be humanely euthanized. Instead they release the animal into the closest wetland or forest to fend for itself. Anyone who has seen a starved house cat in the country knows this is the worst kind of cruelty, yet it occurs all the time. In their pitiful effort to survive, cats absolutely devastate the quail and dove populations and will raid the nests of virtually any kind of bird in reach. They also consume all the lizards, frogs, and small mammals, as well.

One unexpected problem is the dumping of water, fish, and plants from home aquariums into wetland waterways. Exotic fish and water weeds introduced into an ecosystem can have devastating results. Perhaps the worst case is the weed hydrilla. But the fish are a problem, too. Some of the African tropical fish thrive in southeastern swamps and marshes, where they consume less aggressive native fish and amphibians, ultimately disrupting the species balance. In some parts of Florida, this is causing great alarm among fish farmers and wildlife experts.

ODORS Victims of the Mississippi Valley flooding of 1993 will recall the fetid odors of the flood water itself and the mud. Similar odors can be emitted from wetland areas: As the water becomes shallower and warms, mud is exposed, plants decompose, and algae blooms. This is a natural process, but people who live downwind may not appreciate the smells.

FIRE The majority of wetlands are dry for at least part of the year, and many rely on fire as a natural mechanism to keep them healthy. Wetland fires can smoulder for long periods or be fanned by winds into fast-moving wildfires. There is always the threat of fire spreading into nearby neighborhoods. Often kids playing in these wooded areas are the source of ignition.

damage and oversee any control actions. Because even the smallest portion of the plant may be sufficient to start a new colony, it is very difficult to successfully eradicate this weed over the long term. It is also believed that fragments of the plant may be carried by waterfowl as well, so repeated control measures may be required in the future.

Another difficult exotic aquatic weed is water hyacinth, which has been introduced to many of our waterways, where it floats on top. Long roots trail through the water, anchoring the plants in the mud

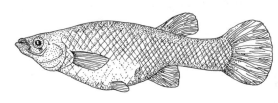

Mosquitofish (Gambusa affinis)

but possibly becoming a serious problem for boats and migratory fish. Hyacinth is not frost-hardy, so it is more prevalent in waterways of the warm-weather states. It was once thought to be a good alternative food for cattle, which caused its introduction into waterways of the west. It is also a popular water garden plant, grown for the attractive succulent foliage and purple flowers.

Hydrilla is spread by bait pails, the props of boat motors, jet skis, water skis, water toys, fishing equipment, beach sand, mud, even in bathing suits—wherever a small portion of the plant can lodge until it is reintroduced into another waterway. Be sure to thoroughly clean anything that can possibly be a carrier of this dreaded aquatic weed. If you suspect hydrilla is present in or around your homesite, contact the nearest USDA Soil Conservation Service or US Fish and Wildlife office for detailed information on containment and control.

4
CREATING A WETLAND HABITAT

Wildlife is one of the lingering reminders of our primitive selves in an increasingly complex and artificial world. As we learn to appreciate the subtleties of nature, we find a deeper appreciation of life. A Pueblo Indian woman once remarked after losing virtually everything she owned, "At least I still have the sunset." And each time I see fiery colors streak across the western sky, I remember her words and know that the most profound wealth we will ever know is free. Yet too many fail to see these subtle signs of the wild things, but with time everyone may come to know them well.

This is what creation and preservation of wetlands is all about. Since we cannot always go out and find the elusive plants and animals we have come to love, we can bring them in with tiny pockets of wetlands. A simplified version of this concept has always been a part of the gardener's world: the backyard birdbath, a seed-filled feeder, and dainty birdhouses hanging from tree branches. These combine to draw in birds with the three requirements of habitat: water, food, and cover.

We have the opportunity to go beyond this contrived version of a wetland by creating more natural habitats on what land is available. A country home, a small farm, or a big backyard is all it takes; the only variable is scale. But first throw away your notions of a controlled water garden or a neatly edged pond because the best shorelines for habitat support a diversity of organisms, from water bugs to field mice, cattails to willow trees. Remember, the most productive wetland is the region *between* dry land and open water.

LARGE-SCALE WETLAND CREATION AND RESTORATION

There are wildlife biologists, landscape architects, civil engineers, and botanists across America actively involved in the huge task of wetland creation and restoration. These are large-scale projects overseen by many government agencies interested in the impact they will have on

Ducks at sunset. (California Department of Water Resources)

wildlife, flood control, pollution, and water availability. Creation of a new wetland is difficult because the hydrology required to keep it functioning properly must be engineered, and in most cases virtually all the plant life must be established by hand. Restoration of a degraded wetland is a bit simpler since the topography, water table, soils, and vegetation may already be in place, though altered. Much of this kind of work involves cleanup of sites, protection, and improvement of water flows to ensure wildlife survival.

There are new laws that forbid diversion of water, dredging, vegetation removal, or other alterations of wetlands without special permits. These restrictions fall under Section 404 of the Clean Water Act and under other laws enforced by the SCS, US Fish and Wildlife, and the EPA. First professionals from federal agencies evaluate a site's soils, vegetation, and hydrology to determine whether it is an official wetland and subject to the regulations protecting wetland habitat. There are often disputes as to the validity of such a designation because there are so many different kinds of situations on private property, both manmade and natural, that could be construed as wetlands and thus be regulated.

Once designated a wetland, the status of a site is determined, and the government then dictates whether any action should be taken to improve it. This sometimes results in undoing what were considered land improvements in the past. One example is the Kissimmee River in Florida, which was straightened and dredged in the 1960s by the Corps of Engineers to improve drainage in the surrounding area. A meandering 43 miles of river channel was streamlined to a straight-shot, 22-mile alignment. Today the Corps is implementing a $372 million project to return the Kissimmee to its original, meandering alignment. This would foster the return of a rich diversity of plant and animal life.

In some cases, these wetland projects are community efforts to improve waterways in and around cities and towns. In the 1800s, riverbanks were often the most common city dumpsites because high water whisked the garbage away. The belief that rivers would dilute industrial pollution also encouraged dumping into rivers. It's not difficult to see how a river could become a disposal mechanism, causing widespread degradation of what could have been the most beautiful aspect of a city. Instead we turned our backs on many sloughs, marshes, ponds, creeks, and rivers, so that today a great number of them are in sorry condition or have simply vanished altogether.

But residents are growing more aware as they learn about the value of wetlands and the enrichment wildlife can bring to our communities. Government agencies concerned with wetlands are eager to help direct and instruct citizens in ways they can help with the process, which is of great benefit to everyone. A town with a beautifully preserved riverfront will be more attractive to new residents and business, thus increasing long-term prosperity. If you have no land to create a wetland of your own, get involved with your community and actively support wildlife refuges, riparian habitat improvement, and wetland restoration efforts however you can.

WETLAND WILDLIFE PROGRAMS

Partners for Wildlife

Much of America's wetlands lies on private property, and in order to involve citizens in protecting or restoring these areas, the US Fish and Wildlife Service has developed the Partners for Wildlife program. It makes the resources and expertise of wetland specialists available to landowners to guide them in identification of habitat areas and ways to ensure they remain in place for future generations. Today there are over 9,000 members of Partners for Wildlife, and the number is growing.

Farmers have traditionally been the ones who own much of our wetland areas, and earlier in this century they were taught to "drain and fill" in order to put more land into cultivation. This has placed many farmers in a bad light as far as environmentalists are concerned, yet most of these agriculturists have grown up on their land and work hard to manage it correctly. The modern farmer realizes the value of wildlife, and dedicating a small acreage to wetlands would have little impact on crop yield. Degraded wetlands can also be returned to their original beauty and productivity with the help of Partners for Wildlife.

A good example of a farmer who supports wildlife is Roger Moore, a rice farmer in the Sacramento Valley. Mallard ducks nest in the rice fields of this valley, and the harvest falls just when the females are sitting on their eggs. Roger grew saddened by the great number of nests gobbled up by the massive combines and decided to do something about it. He developed a plan with a government wildlife biologist because it is illegal to disturb a nest without approval. Roger climbs down off his harvester whenever he sees a nest. He gathers the feather down lining and the eggs, then places them in a white freezer bag, the kind they use at the supermarket. All day Roger stops for the nests to collect the eggs, and at quitting time he brings them home to an incubator. He hatches out the ducklings and raises them in the back yard. When they are old enough, he and the wildlife biologist from the nearby refuge release the young mallards back into the wild. Roger's plan is so successful that neighboring farmers are also slowing harvest to gather eggs, the white freezer bags appearing mysteriously on the doorstep of his house every evening. By the end of the season, Roger can have hundreds of ducklings penned up in his yard waiting for release.

You don't have to be a landowner to join Partners for Wildlife. Individuals and groups can join in order to support this effort in numerous ways. For more information, contact the Wildlife Coordinator at any of the seven US Fish and Wildlife Service regional offices.

North American Waterfowl Management Plan (NAWMP)

This joint venture was established to better coordinate wildlife preservation efforts between Canada and the United States. Migrating water birds can travel long distances between their winter and summer feeding grounds, many of which fall outside our borders. It is difficult for us to effectively preserve and build bird populations when their nesting sites are dwindling in the far north. For example, the estimated loss of wetland habitat in the continental United States is about 50%, while losses in Canada are estimated at over 70% in some important areas.

The management plan focuses on preservation of those wetlands on public lands that are of particular importance to migratory waterfowl. Each year new areas join the project, which already includes the lower Mississippi, the lower Great Lakes, the prairie pothole region, and California's Central Valley. Restoration of wetlands can be a labor-intensive process, and government agencies appreciate any help you can offer. For information on how you can support or become involved in this or other wetland wildlife programs in your area, contact the nearest Fish and Wildlife Service regional office or write: United States Department of the Interior, Fish and Wildlife Service, Arlington Square—NAWMP, 1849 C Street NW, Washington, DC 20240.

YOUR RURAL WETLAND

Many who live in the country would like to see more wildlife activity nearer to home. To sit on the front porch and watch migrating geese float down to rest in your pond is a wonderful experience, and it isn't difficult to encourage such birds to come in. The key is to provide a consistent supply of **water**, **food**, and **cover**.

The most obvious way to begin is to build a farm pond because it offers a visual amenity, recreational potential, and water storage. However, open water is not the most productive wildlife habitat. It is the edges, where the water line fluctuates, that support the greatest diversity of plants and animals.

Building a pond isn't always possible, due to soil type or lack of water. It would surprise you how many disasters occur when inexperienced people try to build ponds. Before you begin, it is essential to contact the nearest USDA Soil Conservation Service. This agency is staffed with experts who can make your project successful and eliminate the all too common failures.

Sometimes poorly designed or constructed ponds become a hazard to people, livestock, and wildlife. For example, one landowner decided to build a 1-acre irrigation pond. Heavy equipment was used to clear the land then dig a fairly nice pond in a ravine, an earth dam on the lowest side. When the winter rains came, the runoff came flowing down into that ravine, carrying loose soil from the newly cleared ground into the pond, which soon overflowed. The silt then moved on downstream to a beautiful, small lake on an adjacent ranch.

The tragedy was that the little lake was a thriving aquatic habitat and contained a huge number of trophy-sized bass treasured by that rancher. The silt filled the lake to a point where the water became so shallow the fish were threatened, and the Soil Conservation Service was called out to assess the damage. Those agents along with wildlife biologists ended up dragging nets through the shallow water to gather the huge fish, then truck them to a river

Although it is not very attractive, this kind of wetland provides water, food, and cover. Food plants abound here, with grains the chief source, and there is plenty of cover to allow small animals access to water without coming into the open. (California Department of Water Resources)

for release. Toward the end of that rigorous day, these devoted agents were wading through the water catching monster fish by hand in an attempt to save every one. Fortunately, they were successful, but the rancher lost his beloved fish, and the inexperienced pond diggers spent weeks excavating the silt from the lake. Despite this repair effort, the rich diversity of life supported by the rancher's pond was utterly destroyed. Needless to say, the diggers were more cautious in the future and utilized the service of the Soil Conservation Service before attempting any more earthwork.

Ponds created for wildlife and aesthetic beauty should look natural. Examples of unnatural ponds include those constructed as reservoirs or farm ponds where water holding is a necessity, not an amenity. A pond should fit comfortably in the folds of the land, with sloping contours tying into the surrounding topography. If material is excavated, these spoils should be evenly distributed around the pond and immediately seeded with erosion-control mixtures or heavily mulched. The more gentle the slopes, the easier it will be for plants to take hold.

Perhaps the most difficult aspect of pond building is the overflow method. If the pond is located in a region of heavy rainfall, or if there is a large amount of runoff draining into it, there must be an overflow. If not, the water spills over and erodes the shoreline at the lowest part and creates a gully, which ultimately lowers the waterline elevation. Two of the most common methods are a well vegetated spillway or outflow pipes, both of which must conform to specific grades and flow ratings. Consult a professional for assistance with an overflow because these can be tricky.

These are just a few important aspects to pond building that must be considered to guarantee success. Some of the most dismal failures are attributed to the following issues.

LEAKING Not all soil types hold water, a fact that has left many empty holes in the ground where a landowner thought a pond should have been. If the soil has fissures or is porous, the water will move through quickly, but slower leaks can be just as much of a problem. It is essential that *before* excavating you have an SCS agent evaluate your pond site to determine its water-holding capacity and whether or not you will be forced to resort to mechanical sealing methods. Sealing a leaky pond of any size is an expensive proposition.

There are only a few options for sealing ponds. For many years civil engineers have depended upon space-age plastics for sealing landfills, toxic waste dumps, and mine tailings. These are ideal for residential ponds, but cost rises with the thickness of the liner. The thicker the liner, though, the less likely animal claws or other sharp objects will puncture it. It's best to hire a professional to select and size the liner for your project.

A naturally occurring pond holds water because there is a very dense, impervious layer of bedrock or clay soil beneath it. This layer can be simulated using clay or bentonite clay, both of which swell when wet to seal and eliminate drainage. If spread in a thick layer over the bottom of the excavated pond, they will simulate a natural condition and increase water-holding capacity. Bentonite, as well as other clays, however, tends to crack when it dries out, thus leaking when water levels fluctuate. It also takes a tremendous amount of this material to seal a pond, and trucking costs can be prohibitive. A less reliable method called **mudcrete** uses a rototiller to combine dry concrete dust in with the soil in the bottom of a newly dug pond. Then it is watered down, and the concrete binds with the soil into a dense but not foolproof layer.

DEPTH One of the biggest problems with water quality is related to water temperature. The

Warm stagnant water can cause serious problems with water weeds and algae bloom in wetlands and ponds. It is a natural part of the eutrophication process, although wetlands in the warm weather states have more of a problem than those of cold weather climates. There is no easy solution. (California Department of Water Resources)

more shallow the pond, the more quickly the water heats up. Warm water coupled with sunlight results in algae bloom and proliferation of aquatic weeds, which can choke a pond, reducing oxygen levels and wildlife diversity. Aquatic weeds as well as algae can be very difficult to remove or control. There is bound to be an accumulation of silt and organic matter, which makes a pond even more shallow over time.

EDGES There is a safety factor to consider as well. Overly steep edges can trap children, pets, and livestock in the pond, making it difficult for them to gain a foothold and climb out. On the other hand, overly shallow edges will support an abundance of reeds such as cattail, which can ring the shoreline in dense vegetation. For wildlife this is a natural edge condition, but it limits access to the water's edge for humans and livestock. This shows how important it is that the edges of the new pond be excavated and graded properly to discourage reed growth and ensure they are safe. The SCS will provide specific guidelines for the proper angle of edging.

If you are trying to coax waterfowl into your pond or wetland, a good idea is to create islands out in the water for nesting sites. The water becomes a protective barrier against predators and domestic animals that disturb nests of ground-nesting birds. Islands should be vegetated with plenty of tall grass and reeds to provide suitable cover.

Seasonal Wetlands

Ponds, with their expanses of water, are attractive and will draw in migratory waterfowl, but we must not forget that most wetlands are seasonal. They may catch and hold water during the rainy season or channel runoff from higher elevations. The water levels will gradually drop from both surface evaporation and percolation into the soil, so that during the dry season there may be no moisture on the surface at all. This cycle from flood to dry and back to flood again is the reason why these wetlands are the most productive habitats, if not always as aesthetically pleasing to us as open water.

These seasonal wetland habitats are easier to create than ponds because there is no need to continually hold water year round. Before you begin, do some research to guide you in how to create the habitat best suited to your region and its wildlife. This means studying regional wildlife to discover what they feed upon and where they breed and nest. Contact your nearest US Fish and Wildlife Service offices, where biologists can help with literature or possibly a site visit. The Soil Conservation Service is also involved with identifying plants that support various species of wildlife and has quite a bit of free literature on the subject. These experts will help you select the ideal site for a seasonal wetland and suggest the best way to adapt it for best results. More importantly, they make sure you don't make irreparable mistakes with grading and drainage.

STEP 1: COLLECT WATER A site conducive to the wetland environment should become a collection point for runoff during the wet season, but not a barrier to drainage. Low-lying ground, gullies, ravines, canyons, and even abandoned drainage ditches are ideal. If earth-moving equipment is available and there is sufficient area, you can create a seasonal wetland by constructing a berm to hold back drainage water. The SCS will assist in sizing the berm to ensure that it remains in place. For smaller projects, dig out the low area by hand and use the earth to create a small berm or dry islands.

In arid climates there is very little water available during the long dry months, making it difficult to create a seasonal wetland. Soils are porous, and the land is parched for most of the year and thus will not support plant life. But creating a water hole is the next best thing, and this method is a more efficient use of water in a drought-prone region. No matter how small a water hole is in the dry country, there's a good chance it will draw in plenty of wildlife, from quail to coyotes. Viewing may be particularly good at night, when species in this climate do most of their foraging. You'll have to keep the water source consistently full, and if possible try to support some grasses or food plants around the edge.

Water-holding methods can be as simple as a slight depression lined with plastic sheeting, but where summer temperatures are high, water holes with a greater surface area will evaporate more quickly. Half of a 50-gallon drum buried to the rim holds lots of water. Even a children's rigid, plastic backyard wading pool is a good choice, and it is long lasting if buried to just below the rim. Use your imagination because virtually anything that is handy will work for this purpose.

STEP 2: SUPPLY FOOD Most species of wildlife spend their time seeking out food. They will come to gather, and are more likely to take up residence, where the food and water supply is abundant. The chief food source is plants that bear seeds, berries, and edible foliage, and those already growing at the site should be saved even if they aren't native. Abandoned fruit trees, winterberry, flowering dogwood, crabapple, mulberry, hawthorn, and oaks are all excellent food-

Barn owls are nocturnal birds of prey that will hunt around wetlands for small rodents that gather there. Standing dead trees, particularly if they are large with hollow centers, are ideal nesting sites for owls. (California Department of Water Resources)

The bald eagle is protected under the Endangered Species Act in the United States because its habitat is shrinking. Like owls and hawks, these birds rely heavily on the wildlife in and around wetlands for food. (California Department of Water Resources)

Mammals are also predators that depend on wetlands and water holes. Common in the western states, coyotes were once considered pests but now are appreciated for their unique niche in the food chain. (California Department of Water Resources)

producing trees. Pyracantha, blackberry, elderberry, grapes, and other vines are all highly productive.

Perennial and annual wildflowers that produce seed can be planted around the edges of a wetland, pond, or water hole to increase its aesthetic beauty while at the same time offering food for birds. Nice selections include Indian pink, goldenrods, coneflowers, Shasta daisy, ironweed, opium poppy, coreopsis, asters, beardtongues, globe thistle, and scarlet sage.

New plants with improved food potential can be sown, such as sunflowers, sorghum, millet, and an assortment of small grains that will sprout on their own in the spring and mature by the time the wetland dries out. Legumes, which include the many clovers, supply highly nutritious greens for rabbits and other small mammals. There is a ready supply of inexpensive seed for leguminous plants because they are used for cover crops by farmers. A simple way to provide food plants is to simply sow wild bird seed around the site.

STEP 3: PROVIDE COVER Cover is important because it gives protection from predators and bad weather. Whether you are supporting a wetland or a smaller source of water, animals of all sorts are most vulnerable when at the water hole, so predators tend to hang around there. Smaller animals need places where they can scurry from one concealed position to another as they approach the water.

Natural cover includes tall grass, twigs, and branches for roosting, as well as shrub thickets, berry brambles, and other types of dense vegetation. That pastoral scene of an open pond surrounded by closely grazed green grass does not provide cover and thus limits use by wildlife. But a water hole or wetland with lots of brush, tall, dry grass, and dead, hollow trees is ideal.

Dead branches or entire trees elsewhere can be cut and planted in postholes to create instant roosting sites. This is a great technique when no trees exist where desired or while waiting for seedling trees to mature. In fact, if this posthole tree is a high point in the landscape, and if there aren't too many other trees nearby, hawks and other raptors may choose to roost there to watch for prey. You can supplement what cover is existing by stacking up some dry brush, mounds of rocks, deposits of bark, or old logs, depending on what is available. Wildlife conservation agencies will also provide you with plans for making nesting boxes for various kinds of birds. Of particular value are den boxes for squirrels and other mammals that occur in your area.

Once your wetland or water hole is in place, it is important to be aware of domestic animals. Cattle, goats, and sheep should not be allowed to graze in the wetland, because they eliminate valuable food plants, affect water quality, and degrade various types of cover. Hungry animals will browse willow and other sweet-barked trees and shrubs vital to reducing erosion. Above all, keep domestic house cats away from this area because they will frighten birds and, in many cases, kill and consume them. Wild house cats reproduce rapidly and can be practically impossible to get rid of except by shooting, but even this is tough because they are elusive and hunt at night. Unvaccinated cats can also carry rabies. You can't keep the cats away with fencing, but most county animal control officers will gladly loan you a live trap.

Establishing Wildlife

A thriving wetland is populated by a broad range of organisms. Plants range from soil fungi to grasses and willows. Insects include tiny larvae and huge dragonflies. Mammals can be as large as a deer or as small as a field mouse. All of these organisms must fit into the food chain somewhere if the area is to be relatively self-sustaining and diverse.

Isolated wetland habitats may have no ready source of wildlife, so you will have to start off the process yourself. The best way to introduce soilborne organisms into your wetland is to find a similar example nearby. From this established site, you can bring a few shovelfuls of mud, which contains seeds, roots, microscopic bacteria, fungi, and even insect eggs lying dormant in the soil. **Do not obtain soil from any recognized wetland, as this is illegal.**

Because algae are also a part of wetlands, a jar of water from another natural site will introduce these water-borne entities. Algae are very simple plants that grow in water and can reproduce into colonies, which are those slimy, floating masses swimmers detest. But like other plants, they feed upon nitrogen and nutrients, which become concentrated in standing water. As these colonies reproduce, age, and die out, decomposition of their organic components consumes oxygen, which is vital to other organisms living in the water. This process of oxygen loss, called **eutrophication**, occurs naturally over a very long period in the evolution of a lake to wet meadow and ultimately to dry land. The process speeds up considerably when the by-products of agriculture and human habitation cause nutrient loading and siltation in a very short time.

In freshwater wetlands, algae are an integral part of the food web, but when present in populations too high, it can severely degrade the habitat. One contributor to algae bloom is an excess in nutrients, deposited in the wetland area by runoff since it is often the lowest point in the landscape. As the concentration increases and the water level grows more shallow, algae find an ideal environment, and a population explosion occurs.

To prevent this problem, be aware of where runoff is originating, particularly during the warm or dry months. In the rainy season the situation eases because nutrient concentrations are diluted and both water and air temperatures are low enough to discourage algae bloom. One of the greatest offenders is livestock, whose manure is full of nitrogen and phosphorus in various forms. Runoff from lawns, irrigated pastures, and ornamental landscapes charged with fertilizers also contributes to the problem. Organisms such as freshwater shrimp, tadpoles, snails, and freshwater clams all feed on algae and may be available in quantity from local aquaculture suppliers. See the resources section of this book for a list. If algae become a serious problem, contact your local SCS office or the nearest county or state agricultural agency for sources and experts.

Mosquitoes are bound to be a problem, but they can be controlled if there are sufficient populations of organisms that prey upon them in either the larval or the adult stage. Mosquito larvae survive only in standing water and thus are most susceptible to fish such as goldfish and guppies. Most mosquito abatement districts or local agricultural agencies can help you obtain mosquitofish, a small minnow known by its Latin name, *Gambusia*. Stocking these types of fish in wetlands, whether permanently or seasonally, cuts way down on the number of adult mosquitoes.

Dragonflies, damselflies, as well as birds and particularly bats are all voracious feeders and consume large numbers of airborne adult mosquitoes. Bats are known to consume up to 600 mosquitoes per hour, and they hunt during the periods when the insects are most active. The easiest way to encourage bats to nest around your wetlands is to build or purchase bat houses, which are widely available from garden supply houses. For more information on these beneficial night fliers, read *America's Neighborhood Bats*, by Merlin D. Tuttle. This charming book dispels old wives' tales of bats as pests and presents them as a beneficial part of many ecosystems.

It can be difficult to get mammals to take up residence in some homemade wetlands, while in others they can become serious pests. Muskrats and other heavy feeders can rapidly consume all the plants you so carefully nurtured.

Beavers can devastate new plantings if there isn't plenty of timber nearby. Next to live trapping, there's not much you can do about them. It's wise to contact a wildlife biologist and discuss your wetland area because these experts are very knowledgeable concerning animals in such places. Your problem mammals can be trapped and released in other wetlands. On the other hand, unwanted mammals taking up residence in urban or high-density areas can sometimes be trapped by fish and game officials and released at your place.

Mammals such as skunks, squirrels, and raccoons are susceptible to rabies, a very dangerous disease transmitted by a bite or scratch from an infected animal. Documented cases of rabid wild and domestic animals is rising in many states but are still somewhat rare. A great number of wild animals are nocturnal, but when rabid they will wander around in broad daylight. Any such unusual sighting should be reported to animal control authorities.

Another disease, plague, is transmitted by the bite of a flea. These fleas will hop off the dead body of a wild animal such as a ground squirrel and hop onto a household pet. If that flea should bite a human, infection results. Plague has become a problem in western campgrounds where squirrels and chipmunks are half-tame and feed off the leavings of campers. Often the fleas infest household pets brought along.

Establishing Plants

There are many different species of plants growing in wetlands of varying depths. Some are particularly aggressive and always become dominant, whether they are native or exotics introduced from other continents. Cattails, bulrush, and reed grass are all native but invasive, and you may have to keep them weeded out so more desirable plants can develop to provide better food and cover for wildlife. Before planting or removing anything from a wetland, contact your local experts to obtain a clear picture of how the wetland should be vegetated.

It is simple to plant seed or cuttings of riparian vegetation around the drier fringes of a wetland, but introducing aquatic plants can be difficult. Some very simple methods used by experts are quite effective on a smaller scale. The most common is the use of a clay **sinker**. This is nothing more than a big ball of clay attached to the roots of a plant and literally dropped right into the water. Clay is so dense it is heavy enough for the plant to sink to the bottom right-side up every time. Clay won't dissolve very quickly underwater, either, and it can also hold down buoyant seed. In shallower water, plants may be planted by hand in the soft mud.

5
SOIL EROSION AND SILTATION

Water is one of the most powerful elements in nature. It has carved out the Grand Canyon, washed away shorelines, and sculptured solid granite into exotic forms, all by the gradual wearing away of rock and soil. Although we can easily see the effects of water in these examples, the really damaging erosion occurs by runoff flowing down ditches and gullies or fanning out in a shallow sheet over hundreds of acres. When there is sufficient rainfall to cause flooding, this erosive force is compounded by the massive amount of water, its high rate of speed, and its turbulence.

Two basic effects of rainwater are splash and runoff. Understanding how these occur and where they are likely to cause problems helps you better prepare for flooding and perhaps prevent smaller scale soil loss in the future.

SPLASH Each time a raindrop falls upon the earth, it dislodges a few tiny soil particles. When many raindrops fall, the amount of disturbed soil is significant. Engineers calculate that the energy of raindrops falling on an acre of land at a rate of 0.1 ($^1/_{10}$) inch an hour is equal to roughly 100 horsepower. Raindrops falling on that same acre at 2 inches an hour equals 250 horsepower. At 2 inches an hour, this force is sufficient to lift a 7-inch-deep topsoil layer to a height of 3 feet a total of 86 times during an hour's rain, equivalent to 518 million foot-pounds of work.

The rain caused by summertime thunderstorms can be the most damaging because it falls heavily in a very short time. Originally, natural vegetation such as prairie sod, brush, and forests covered most of the land, acting as a natural check against the erosive forces of these storms. When the early farmers stripped the land, it was left unprotected from the direct impact of raindrops. Water splashed freely upon the bare soil to erode away its surface, then ran off at great velocity to carry even more of the earth away. The results of this were evident in the great Dust Bowl of the 1930s, which was a product of long-term erosion followed by drought and wind. What this tells us is that soil protected by plants is less likely to suffer splash erosion.

RUNOFF When rain first begins to fall, some of the water percolates into the soil, but once the soil is saturated or if the rain is falling faster than the rate of absorption, runoff will result. Runoff always flows downhill, even if the tilt of the land is slight, and it gathers at the lowest points in the watershed, usually lakes and rivers. If runoff is greater than these waterways can accommodate, however, a flood event occurs and the overflow becomes uncontrolled.

Runoff may become channelized into ditches, streams, or gullies, either natural or manmade, on its journey to low land. It can also spread out into shallow sheet flows that cover very large areas of flat land, if there isn't enough variation in the topography to cause channelization. When water flows over land, its movement picks up soil particles just as a splashing raindrop does, which is why flood waters tend to be so muddy in color. When these waters encounter irregularities, a circular, wavelike scouring effect is produced and will become increasingly pronounced when water is moving more quickly.

The **velocity**, or speed, at which water is flowing is expressed in feet per second. The greater the velocity of moving water, the more pressure that is exerted upon any object in its path. **Slow-moving** flood water is flowing at a velocity of less than 3 feet per second and inflicts minimal erosion upon the soil. Water moving faster than this rate scours the soil over which it flows and causes serious erosion. Not only does it carry away fertile topsoil, fast-moving water can erode the base soil beneath levees, undermine foundations, and uproot large trees as the soil binding the roots is washed out. You can see firsthand the effects of mild scouring in the small rills and gullies created in sandy streambanks where the water is flowing slowly. Not only does scouring pick up soil with the moving water, it also carries it off suspended in the water until velocity slows enough for the particles to drop out. These deposits are called **silt** or **sediment**.

In heavy clay there is less scouring because this type of soil holds tightly together. There is a greater incidence of scouring on sand, which has very little cohesiveness. Highly organic soil containing a lot of humus is usually the source of fertile silt deposits left behind on the flood plain after water recedes. This is the most valuable silt, and it has enriched flood plains since the beginning of time, yet it robs the surrounding uplands to do so.

When extreme flooding occurs with great turbulence and high flow velocity, the flood plain can be left riddled and scarred. Topsoil may be absent in some places, and great deposits may be left in others. Homesites in flood plains are vulnerable to both scouring and silt deposits. If your home is located where the water slows down, mounds of sediment and debris can end up in your yard. The origins of the sediments in flood waters can vary considerably and don't always contribute fertile soil, as is widely believed. If the material originated from sandy deposits, for example, it may afford little benefit.

In arid climates or at the headwaters of major rivers, the water is usually channeled by hilly terrain. With heavy flows, turbulence increases the scouring along the

The erosive powers of fast-moving flood waters are capable of great destruction. (California Department of Water Resources)

70

banks of these waterways. These banks tend to contain high amounts of gravel, which is carried but a short distance if at all. Rocks don't usually become suspended in flowing water unless it is a violent rapid. Instead, they roll gradually down the riverbed. Rapids so enjoyed by river rafters are a result of the erosive force of flood water scouring the sides of canyons until they collapse into the river. Water shoots up the face of a midstream boulder, then falls turbulently down the other side to create a rapid. The power of water falling has tremendously erosive scouring forces, similar to those of ocean waves of the beach.

During flooding, any interruption in the riverbed or ground plain, like a building or depressions such as irrigation ditches or ponds, will cause scouring. These effects will not be visible until the water recedes, but the predictability of such action is well known by civil engineers. Their designs for improvements to rivers or inside floodways always take scouring into consideration.

Erosion can occur on soil that is not inundated with flood water. Newly cleared or disturbed land sheds a tremendous amount of silt into the watershed drainage. Over a few decades there can be considerable filling of riverbeds and drainage ditches, which reduces their capacity. This then inhibits drainage and increases the chance of future flooding, because water will more quickly overflow the shallower ditch or river during peak flows.

During periods of low flows, the boulders that create rapids are visible in river beds. These cause the wave-like action and increased turbulence that scour.

There is more than just silt transported in flood waters. Rapidly flowing water in the main currents can pick up and move chunks of ice, trees, portions of buildings, and other debris, which increase the erosion potential as they bounce along and loosen the riverbed or slam into stationary objects.

Perhaps the greatest example of this filling in and decreased capacity is the devastation following the hydraulic mining boom which spanned the 1850s to 1880s. This destructive method used huge water cannons to dissolve entire hillsides in an effort to extract gold from ancient river sediment. The water and thousands of cubic tons of tailings were dumped back into the rivers, which

71

devastated the riparian and wetland ecosystems they supported. The rivers filled and became so shallow they could no longer be navigated, and the flooding became more frequent and turbulent. The water also deposited sand and gravel upon rich farmland in the river bottoms, forever burying their fertile soil.

So great was this filling of the river channels with tailings that levees far downstream had to be built higher in order to accommodate the runoff. Even today, more than a hundred years later, the impact of these tailings still mars the riparian wetlands along many rivers. So great was the nineteenth-century devastation that the federal government enacted strict mining laws to prohibit tailing dumping into rivers, some of the earliest environmental legislation in the United States.

Because every drop of rain that falls upon our home or land must flow *somewhere*, usually to a drainage ditch or a river, we must all be aware of both the potential for erosion and the inevitable points where suspended silt will eventually settle out. Even in the city, underground storm drains end up dumping into rivers or the ocean. Erosion sediment can cause damage to these bodies of water as well, and accumulation in a storm drain system can greatly reduce its capacity.

SEDIMENT AND WETLANDS

Perhaps the most tragic result of siltation is the degradation of wetlands. As discussed in other chapters, many wetlands are in a state of transition, somewhere in the natural process of succession. The problem is that the gradual filling of wetlands with sediment, which can naturally take many centuries or more to complete, is speeded up a thousand times by erosion from human sources. Sediment can also clog or alter the course of drainages, which results in flooding of new areas, often with disastrous results. With erosion and sedimentation being the sources of such widespread problems both in terms of wildlife habitat and flood control, it is important we know how our actions can aggravate the problem.

PLANTS AND EROSION CONTROL

Nature and experience have proved that plants are the ideal means of controlling or reducing erosion. Plants protect the soil surface from the direct battering of raindrops and diffuse the impact of each drop by scattering it over a greater area. Plant roots bind the soil and hold it together even when saturated. The aboveground portions of plants, particularly trees and shrubs, act as barriers or small checkdams to slow the velocity of runoff. Plants in watersheds catch and consume water, reducing the amount of runoff downstream.

In the nineteenth and early twentieth centuries, country roads often had to cross perennially wet, low-lying ground. This was a problem for both wagons and automobiles, which easily became bogged down in the muck. A popular

THE MOST COMMON SOURCES OF EROSION

GROUND RECENTLY CLEARED OF VEGETATION, OR "GRUBBED OUT" This includes removal of trees or shrub cover and grasses. Loss of vegetative cover not only leaves soil vulnerable to erosion, it creates a greater volume of runoff, which must be considered downstream from the site.

FRESHLY GRADED SOIL This is ground that has been recontoured by heavy equipment for house pads, lawns, or parking lots. In most cases, grading cannot be accomplished in a single day, leaving the site vulnerable to erosion if rainfall occurs. In some cases, rain will leave the site too muddy to work for some time, which extends the length of time that untreated, newly exposed soil is highly subject to erosion.

Construction projects are a big source of silt in runoff. Here expanses of newly graded soil are exposed to the splash erosion of rainfall and the scouring effects of the runoff.

CUT SLOPES In the act of cutting a new slope, subsoil previously covered with topsoil becomes exposed. Some types, such as sand and gravel strata, are highly susceptible to erosion and will disintegrate with even a small amount of runoff. Saturation can destabilize the slope to the extent that damaging mudslides can occur. To avoid problems it is wise to divert runoff and install permanent drainage features to keep a slope adequately stable.

FILL SLOPES In most cases, a 95% compaction rate is required on any pad created with fill material. Sometimes the fill material may originate from different sites, which varies the soil density within the pad, and water tends to seek out these changes as flow lines. Elevated-earth building pads are frequently used to floodproof homes within designated flood plains, and when saturated they can sag or disintegrate around the edges from wave action.

WATER RUNOFF CHANNELED INTO UNPROTECTED GULLIES OR DITCHES Runoff can move rapidly, particularly in steeper terrain. This is a serious problem with flash flooding because the velocity contributes to erosion and scouring. In arid climates the gullies may be dry for most of the year, but when flooded suddenly, the banks may suffer undermining. It takes only a short time in some soils for a small drainage depression to become a gaping trench. For bank stabilization methods, refer to chapter 2.

ROADS AND DRIVEWAYS There are often problems with gravel roads or driveways improperly constructed and thus susceptible to erosion. This is more common in hill country, where roadways of any sort should be graded to allow for drainage. Attempts to cross wet or dry stream beds without culverts always result in washout or scouring. Roads without ditches or swales along the edges will accumulate water in the roadway and cause potholes or

Runoff channeled into a single area can erode the banks very quickly. This arrangement of sandbags helps keep the banks intact and reduce further disintegration and widening of the gully. Sheet plastic laid out on the flow line cuts down on scouring, which can make the gully deeper very quickly. (California Department of Water Resources)

deep mud. Roadbeds of all roads or driveways must conform to one of these drainage methods: a) roadbed is crowned in the center and drains down to ditches on both shoulders; b) roadbed is tilted to either one side or the other, where a ditch collects the runoff; or c) in wet ground the entire roadbed is raised above the surrounding terrain, and drainage may be shed to one or both sides.

custom was to plant the wet ground with dense groves of melaleuca, poplar, and other trees known to take up a large amount of moisture through their roots. It was believed the trees would drink up the moisture to render the ground drier, but this did not prove as successful as first thought. Perhaps the worst effect was that these greedy trees naturalized and invaded the surrounding countryside. In Florida, melaleuca, an Australian native, has become a serious pest tree. It has overwhelmed sensitive swamp ecosystems on a massive scale to greatly reduce wildlife diversity and degrade habitat.

CONTROLLING TOPSOIL EROSION Prairie sod was once very thick, not like the thin stuff used to sod a lawn. It proved an ideal cover for large expanses of very windy, treeless plain that could receive a high amount of rainfall in a very short time. Surface-erosion-control plants, such as grasses, clovers, sedges, and other herbaceous seed plants, make up most soil-holding seed mixtures. Annual rye is usually included because it germinates in a matter of days and promises quick coverage until perennial plants mature. These late-coming perennials will crowd out the rye to become the predominant stand.

Sites experiencing periodic flooding suffer from pits and scars of scouring and require a very strong network to hold the surface under such abuse. One of the best plant groups is the runner grasses; they can be highly invasive, but it is precisely this tenacity that is needed in flood plains. Bermuda grass, Adalayd, and other spreading varieties are ideal and have proven to be effective in many cases. They also hold banks and shorelines because they root as they travel and are resistant to breakage. If pieces are broken off by the current, these may lodge elsewhere on the bank and take root.

Topsoil erosion on sloping ground can also be controlled with ground-cover plants, particularly those consisting of many individuals. They typically do not have the rooting depth of the seed plants, but they offer a greater diversity of foliage types and flowers.

SUBSOIL EROSION When soil becomes saturated to a considerable depth, it loses its cohesive qualities. If this occurs on sloping ground, the soil creeps or slides, as is often seen on levee banks. This differs from surface erosion because it occurs deep in the soil and remains invisible at first. Only after there has been some serious movement will surface cracking appear or actual mudslides result.

CREEP is a very gradual movement of soil, which may take years to become visible. But creep can destabilize foundations and crack concrete slabs. Slides are more obvious because they tend to occur all at once and involve large masses of earth. Creep and slides are the sources of problems on raised building pads of compacted fill material and on cut-and-fill lots. They also threaten levees and dikes of all sizes, both public and privately owned. The chances of both occurring is increased by long-term inundation or when drainage is improperly channeled toward sloping ground.

In some cases, planting deep-rooted, soil-binding trees and shrubs will reduce the tendency for slides. However, before planting anything on a levee or a flood berm, contact the office of your nearest Army Corps of Engineers or Soil Conservation Service. Levees can be degraded by vegetation, and the project should be approved by flooding authorities *prior* to selecting plants or digging the first hole.

For most other types of sloping ground, however, trees and shrubs present an inexpensive method of stabilization. Species with a vast network of fibrous roots are the most effective because the roots act like a giant net to integrate the soil. Plants with long, deep taproots can actually cause problems because these thick roots become conduits allowing water to move far into the slope.

≣≣≣

The USDA Soil Conservation Service has regional offices nationwide staffed with experts on soil erosion. Simply give them a call or write a letter expressing your needs. They may provide you with appropriate informational materials and an erosion control plan, as well as suggest sources for obtaining plants. In addition, they may decide that mechanical means of helping plants get started may be essential on certain difficult sites, a factor that can save you money and increase long-term success.

≣≣≣

Planting Techniques

Annual plants germinate quickly from seed and are the best erosion control method for a variety of reasons. For the flat or mildly sloping sites so often found in flood plains, mechanical drill seeding is a good way to sow large areas. Drill seeders are widely available, being used for planting field crops, and they sow a sizable tract evenly in a very short time.

Ground too steep for drill seeders can be sown by hand or with a technique called **hydroseeding** or **hydromulch**. This is simply a tank truck filled with a fibrous mulch, seed, and water mix shot at high pressure onto virtually any surface. If a slope is unusually steep, an organic glue called a **tackifier** holds the seed in place much longer. You will find hydroseeding contractors or drill seeding outfits in your yellow pages, or inquire with SCS, who will direct you to one.

Mechanical Erosion Controls

There are many different kinds of mechanical controls for immediate, if temporary, reduction of erosion on newly disturbed sites, such as newly burned watersheds, construction sites, large grading projects, and excavations. In many cases, these mechanical controls become permanent as part of the overall erosion control revegetation program. Refer to chapter 2 for more information on mechanical revetment and bank erosion control.

The goals of mechanical erosion control techniques:

1. To immediately protect exposed soil from the erosive splash of raindrops and reduce the subsequent runoff.

LIVESTOCK AREAS

Some of the most damaging sources of eroded sediment are livestock areas. Next time you drive through the countryside, note how all the vegetation in some fenced corrals or pens is grazed away to nothing, leaving just the bare earth. Outside the fence there are usually plenty of weeds and grass. The soil in some of these areas also suffers from compaction from livestock hoof-traffic, which makes the soil nearly as hard as concrete. This causes a greater amount of runoff, which flows at increased velocity. Not all of the enclosure will be packed to the same density, and those areas of looser soil will be subjected to scouring and erosion. In many cases, this is the cause of gully formation in livestock pastures, where the runoff becomes channeled. If this runoff drains straight into streams, wetlands, or ditches, the silt will drop out and fill these drainages.

It is important to always retain a buffer zone of weeds or grasses between the enclosure and waterways or wetlands. This vegetation acts as a filter to catch sediment, diffuse channelization, and slow the velocity. This is also very important wherever livestock have access to natural streams or rivers because they tend to congregate near the water sources. This results in compaction and subsequent erosion along the banks, which can literally destroy a river channel. Livestock also feed heavily on vegetation, which serves many important functions. It is critical habitat for wildlife, and plants filter out debris, slow flow rates, and decrease bank erosion in times of high water. A second problem with livestock is the concentrations of nitrates which enter the runoff from concentrations of manure.

2. To slow the velocity of water flowing over the surface and thus reduce the potential for scouring.
3. To filter silt moving with the water and to cause it to settle out more quickly, preferably before it leaves the site.
4. To use absorbent materials, which hold a greater amount of runoff and help soils retain water that would otherwise become runoff.
5. To provide nooks and crannies suitable for germination of erosion control plant seed.

The following represent some of the most commonly used mechanical erosion control materials for immediate effect. Some, such as geotextiles and gunite (concrete) treatments, are not listed because they are prohibitively expensive. However, for extreme conditions such as a home on the edge of a collapsing streambank, field professionals may feel one of these more costly methods is the only secure choice. Fortunately, the majority of means available are quite affordable.

PLASTIC SHEETING Sheets of plastic are a successful means of separating rainfall and runoff from the soil. They protect the surface against raindrop splash and, if properly anchored, divert runoff and keeps the soil reasonably dry. But the plastic does not hold up long, tearing if battered by winds or debris. Sheeting is frequently used on levees with sandbags to reduce the amount of rainfall hitting the sloping outside surface. It is also helpful where wave action or oversaturation is threatening elevated-earth building pads, or where flash flooding has further undermined streambanks that are eroding quickly and threatening homes. In most flood conditions, sandbags must be used to hold the plastic in place. Sheeting accomplishes erosion control goal 1 above.

STRAW MULCH This is the all-purpose, emergency erosion control material. Bales are easy to stack and transport, plus they are so tightly bound that once opened, the amount of resulting loose straw is surprising. Perhaps one of the best qualities of straw is that it is purely organic, breaking down into soil-building organic matter. Straw surface mulch is an excellent surface filter for erosion; if punched into wet ground with a shovel or boot, it will stay put. This punching also provides an ideal environment for seeds to take root, but be sure to sow seed only after the mulch is in place.

A general rule of thumb is to allow about 2 tons of straw per acre of exposed ground, distributed in a layer about 3 inches thick. On steeper ground, SCS field agents may recommend a covering of biodegradable jute or wood excelsior mesh, but in a pinch you can use chicken wire or field fence to hold the straw in place. Later on, the wire coverings must be removed, while the organic netting will simply decompose. Straw accomplishes goals 1 to 5.

MESH AND NETTING Jute mesh is simply twine woven into a giant net, used to stabilize slopes and help seed plants to germinate. It also holds cut shale-type slopes, which shed stones and rock fragments. Wood excelsior mesh, another type of lightweight netting, is made of wood by-products mixed with plastic, but it is not as strong or long lasting as jute. Photodegradable plastic netting is also available; while not organic in origin, it disintegrates under exposure to direct sunlight and the elements. Netting accomplishes goals 2, 3, and 5.

6
EMERGENCY PROCEDURES AND DIGGING OUT

Over the past 2 years, there has been record flooding in the midwestern and southern states. In many communities, residents who had never seen flooding before were caught totally unprepared for the dangerous conditions and total devastation left in the wake of such high water. There are many factors contributing to this problem, some of them well documented in the preceding chapters. But there are likely to be more flood events in these areas, as well as in other states not widely known to be at risk, because of increased runoff due to the following:

1. Wetlands filled or drained for agriculture or development no longer hold excess flood waters.

Aerial view of flooded farmland. (California Department of Water Resources)

2. Levee systems, particularly those under private ownership, are aging.
3. Silt deposits in rivers and streams have reduced capacity, requiring higher levees to contain flows.
4. Paved surfacing has increased. Paving has no ability to absorb runoff, and thus almost 100% of all rainwater falling upon such areas becomes runoff.
5. Over the last few decades, development has encroached into flood plains, resulting in a greater number of homes in high-risk areas.
6. Population increase forces more land to be turned to development.

MAKING PLANS BEFORE THE FLOOD

Our most common flood events are classified as **riverine**. This means that rainfall or snow-melt occurring at any point in a watershed will have an impact on waterways and communities located downstream. The further downstream you go, the more water there is pouring into the main river from its many tributaries. This is why flooding in coastal areas, particularly when coupled with storm tides and high winds, can be so devastating, as the greatest volume of water is concentrated there.

To get a better idea of how this compounded flooding behaves close to the coastline or a lake, think of the river mouth as a storm drain grate along a street curb. The pavement on every side of the grate has been graded to drain to this single point. Each of the flow lines may not contain much water, but when combined there is a huge volume. Should a few leaves become clogged in the grate, the water backs up. This is similar to what happens when storm tides on the coast back up into city storm drains. The pressure at the drain can equal the pressure of the tide pushing up through the pipe in the opposite direction. An equilibrium results, so the water just sits there, accumulating to flood low-lying areas until the forces of tide and runoff are altered. The more water flowing into this bottleneck, the higher the flood level.

Riverine flooding can begin far upstream when storms or thaws occur suddenly at the headwaters. This view shows how a river changes as it drops in elevation from hill country down alluvial fans to flat land.

Imagine this situation inland, where the runoff is filling a major river like the Mississippi; identical conditions may afflict smaller rivers and streams in virtually every state. Much of the Mississippi is lined with great earth levees on both sides, some 50 feet high. Water from rain far upstream accumulates like a freeway at rush hour, with everyone trying to merge into lanes at once. Cars keep coming from each on-ramp, even though the traffic has slowed to bumper to bumper. A river under these conditions does not stop, as we must

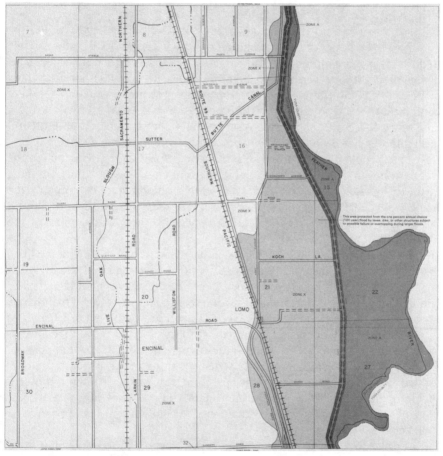

This is an actual FIRM prepared for Sutter County, California on the flood plain of the Feather River. It is similar to those prepared for other communities which are part of the NFIP. On this map the river defines the eastern edge of the map. The land between the river and the levee is shaded darkest and defined in the legend as the A Zone or 100-year flood plain. It is also the Special Flood Hazard Area (SFHA). The area on the outside of the levee is shaded lighter and defines the X Zone or 500-year flood plain. The remaining area of the map is not indicated as being at risk of flooding.

in an automobile. Rivers simply rise if levees are in place, or they spread out over the natural flood plain.

Authorities measure flood events by their **rate of rise**. It is important to know this in order to predict when a community will be inundated or the time in which it will take a flood to reach the top of a levee. All emergency efforts are centered on the rate of rise, in order to schedule evacuations and station crews to shore up levees. The **flood crest** is the level where the river ceases to rise and begins to gradually recede. Should there be repeated rainfall or similar events within the watershed, there may be more than one crest, varying somewhat in their final heights.

If you live in a flood-prone community, knowing the rate of rise and the crest helps you better understand ahead of time what the flood water is likely to do. This is more difficult in arid climates, where flash flooding occurs suddenly, often without warning. At night or when the rainfall is far away, residents can be completely unaware of the rapidly growing threat. Many of these communities flood so rarely they do not need levees, which contributes to a false sense of security. As a result, residents fail to heed safety precautions, and flash flooding has been the cause of an unusually high rate of deaths.

Some people have lived in the same homes for decades, oblivious to the fact that they lie in a long-forgotten high-water zone. These are the ones most likely to be taken unaware when that 500-year flood rises to inundate the home. Your local city or county offices may have records on historic floods. Begin with the public works department because they handle most of the urban and suburban storm drain systems.

If your community has joined the National Flood Insurance Program (NFIP), there will be Flood Insurance Rate Maps (FIRM) covering all of the high-risk areas in and around the 100-year flood plain. There will be areas identified as Special Flood Hazard Areas; residents within these zones are required to purchase flood insurance, as mandated by the Flood Disaster Protection Act of 1973.

The NFIP is a valuable service established in 1968 to help reduce the disaster relief funds needed in communities experiencing repeated flooding. In the past, local and sometimes entire state economies of these areas were devastated and grew progressively incapable of recovering. Another problem obtaining flood insurance was the exorbitantly high cost of coverage in communities sure to flood again. Residents had virtually no means of protecting themselves.

In order to improve these areas and encourage them to implement flood control measures, the federal government created the NFIP. It combines private insurance companies with federal resources to spread the cost of insurance over the entire nation, rather than concentrating it in the flood zones. In order to set this program in motion, studies were made to generate flood-risk data and maps delineated to indicate where inundation was most likely and at what frequency and depth. These maps are available to residents and remain on file with local government offices. Maps will tell exactly where a home or land is located in terms of the 100-year base flood elevation (BFE). In some cases, a 500-year mark is indicated as well, because a surprisingly large proportion of the flood damage claims come from the area between the 100- and 500-year elevations.

Buy Flood Insurance

Homeowner's and renter's insurance policies do not usually cover flooding. Often the only way to obtain flood insurance coverage is to buy a separate policy under the National Flood Insurance Program, but this is available only to participating communities. If you are located in a Special Flood Hazard Area (SFHA) as indicated by the maps, you may be eligible for coverage of a home, condominium, business, farm, or permanently installed mobile home. This isn't limited just to homeowners, because renters can also insure their personal property as long as the dwelling is in insurable condition and located within a participating community. There are also programs available that reimburse homeowners for costs involved with floodproofing a home.

Policies may be purchased from any licensed property insurance agent or broker in good standing with the state. There is a process you must follow before the flood insurance policy is final and accepted by the Federal Emergency Management Agency:

1. A property owner perceives a risk of flooding to an insurable building and elects to purchase flood insurance, or a lender making a mortgage informs the builder or potential buyer that the building is in a Special Flood Hazard Area (SFHA) and flood insurance is required.
2. The owner, builder, or borrower contacts an insurance agent or broker to underwrite the policy.
3. The insurance agent completes the necessary forms.
4. The builder or buyer obtains an elevation certificate completed by a licensed engineer, architect, surveyor, or appropriate community official.
5. The insurance agent submits the application, necessary elevation certification, and full premium to the NFIP company. If the application is to cover an existing home, the premium is paid to the insurance company.

There are a number of factors determining the rate charged for a policy under the NFIP. These include aspects of the house itself, such as location, elevation in the flood plain, age, and design. It also depends on the amount of coverage purchased on the house and the number of occupants. There are other regulations based on the amount of money loaned on a home or building, and whether the community is in the emergency or regular phase of the program. Emergency phase coverage is limited and available soon after the community begins working with the NFIP. The regular phase, with higher coverage, is available after a detailed flood study has been prepared for the community. Be on the safe side and contact a reputable insurance agent in your community to discuss all the rules and regulations of the NFIP and annual premium for coverage.

Flood control officials warn that unverified information and misleading statements often lead to disaster. The Tennessee Valley Authority has a good record for consumer information regarding flooding. They recommend the following:

1. Do not rely on assurances that the construction of flood control works has eliminated flooding. The construction of flood control works is not practical in reducing flooding on most streams.
2. Don't accept statements from present owners, neighbors, or sellers that a site has never flooded or that the flood problem has been "fixed."
3. Always check with local building officials *before* you buy a home or homesite. Seek assistance in determining whether a flood hazard exists with a building inspector, city or town manager, planner, engineer, code of enforcement officer, or agent of the NFIP.
4. Do not consider the lack of detailed flood *data* to mean the absence of flood *hazard*, and never rely on property appraisals to determine flood hazard.
5. Never forget that all streams, regardless of size, will overflow their banks and flood if it rains long and hard enough.
6. It can be difficult if not impossible to sell property that has been damaged by flood waters or is identified as being in a flood hazard area.
7. Not every community is participating in the national flood insurance program, so be sure to verify participation before purchasing land or a home.

Awareness: Weather, Flood Warnings, Public Announcements

There are two types of flooding: **flash flooding** occurs up to 6 hours after the rain event; **flooding** is a longer term event, maybe lasting a week or more.

There is usually plenty of time to prepare for flooding, but you must stay tuned to local radio or television stations for current conditions. Nearly half of all flash flooding deaths are auto-related, with motorists caught unaware by flood water or underestimating the danger of shallow flood water. Attempts to cross flooded arroyos or washes or

During normal flood events water rises slowly and may reach the top of the levee—as seen here—without any serious threat. In fact, loads of sightseers often walk the levees to view the flooding. Such sightseeing becomes a hindrance to levee inspectors and repair equipment.

NFIP COVERAGE TIPS

Some Types of Property and Items *Not* Covered by the NFIP

Buildings over water	Gas and liquid storage tanks
Livestock	Aircraft
Birds	Wharves and docks
Fish	Piers
Shrubbery	Land only (without dwelling)
Motor vehicles	Machinery or equipment in the open
Swimming pools	Boats
Floodwalls	Driveways
Crops	Landscaping
Fences	Wind-driven rain damage

Damage due to high groundwater backup into sewers

Flood insurance covers both the home and its contents. It is wise to compile and maintain a room-by-room inventory of the insured contents with either a video or still camera, and store the film off site. Save receipts or a record of the manufacturer, serial number, model number, price, and date and place of purchase when buying major appliances. Keep your insurance policies and a list of personal property in a safety deposit box or somewhere located on high ground.

to drive down city streets carrying fast-moving water are both dangerous and should never be attempted. Often the actual depth of the water is uncertain. If a roadway has been washed out, there may be very deep pockets hidden beneath the level surface of the stream. It is better to turn around and find another route rather than attempt to cross. If your car stalls while traveling through a flooded area, the water may continue to rise and engulf the vehicle. It is best to get out of the car immediately and leave it behind before you get caught.

A mere 2 feet of flood water flowing at 6 to 12 miles an hour can carry away most automobiles. Television rescue programs frequently deal with flash flooding, featuring drivers of four-wheel-drive trucks who mistakenly believe they can plow through flood waters. Most fail to realize the buoyancy of any vehicle increases with the depth of the water; for each foot the water rises, the vehicle weighs *1,500 pounds less.*

Should you encounter flooding at any time, move quickly to higher ground and do not approach the water. The level may rise unexpectedly and trap those within its reach. **Never try to cross a flowing stream of water on foot if the depth is above your ankles.**

Before, during, and after flood events, local emergency management agencies (EMAs) frequently broadcast reports from the National Weather Service (NWS) on current and forecasted flood conditions. The broadcasts can be heard on radio, TV, and NOAA Radio, a special frequency used by the National Oceanic and Atmospheric Administration. If power is cut off from your community during the flood, you will need a battery-operated radio or TV to continue hearing the broadcasts.

These agencies will be using the following important terms to describe where flooding is to occur and the type of flood conditions you can expect.

FLASH FLOOD OR FLOOD WATCH Flash flooding or flooding is possible within the designated watch area. Be alert and ready to evacuate at a moment's notice, and do so immediately after the official order.

FLASH FLOOD OR FLOOD WARNING Flash flooding or flooding has been reported or is imminent. Take necessary precautions at once and act quickly. Unlike with some other disasters, staying behind serves no practical purpose and is very dangerous. It is essential you get out of the area before you are cut off by flood water.

URBAN AND SMALL STREAM ADVISORY Flooding of small streams, streets, and low-lying areas, such as railroad underpasses and urban storm drains, is occurring.

FLASH FLOOD OR FLOOD STATEMENT This is follow-up information regarding a flash flood or flood event.

The Basic Components of a Family Disaster Plan

Every family should be prepared for floods with a disaster plan created ahead of time. Parents and children should know exactly what to do because this reduces the danger and helps everyone remain calm. Panic and fear are the greatest enemies during such stressful times.

Begin by gathering information about flooding hazards in your area. Learn whether there is a risk of flash flooding and know the average flood depth, the average duration, and the frequency of such events. Know how your community deals with flooding and where the nearest high ground is.

Arrange a meeting place on high ground and, if possible, identify a second location as well. Determine the best way to get there from home, school, or business on roads that do not go through low areas. Arrange a place for pets and livestock above the floodway, such as other farms or a kennel. Identify a friend's home outside the area that can become a family "message center." If members of the family are separated, there may be no way to contact each other, but with the message center everyone may call in their status.

This flooded home shows just how deep the water can get. It serves no purpose to remain behind after evacuation orders. Homes as badly flooded as this one may be condemned after the waters recede, which means the residents will have to "camp out" until a new home is found. (California Department of Water Resources)

When the order comes to evacuate, it is essential you be prepared to do so at a moment's notice. For this reason, keep your auto gasoline tank at least half full to be sure there's enough to get you to safety. Knowing what to take in an evacuation makes the situation easier, and you should keep a fully stocked survival kit at all times. Remember that you may be away from home for a week or more, and if your house has been flooded, it will take a long time to dry it out and make repairs. In most disaster areas the stores may also be involved in the flood, and those not flooded may run out of essentials very quickly. The more complete your survival kit, the more able your family will be to cope with the emergency. Store these items in a strong, easily carried container, backpack, or duffel bag. You may also keep these and other emergency equipment in the trunk of your car or at another location on high ground.

List #1 Family Survival Kit
- A 3-day supply of water, allowing 1 gallon per person per day
- Packaged food that won't spoil without refrigeration (food not requiring cooking will be the most versatile)
- One change of clothes and an extra pair of shoes for each person

- One blanket or sleeping bag per person
- First aid kit
- Portable radio (battery operated)
- Flashlight
- Extra batteries
- Extra set of car keys
- Credit card or spare cash
- Prescription drugs and other medications
- A mess kit with paper cups, plates, and plastic utensils
- Infant care items, such as formula and diapers
- Manual can opener
- Utility knife
- Toilet paper
- Hand soap and detergent
- Feminine supplies
- Supplies for dentures and contact lenses
- Rain gear
- Whistle
- Entertainment, such as games and books
- Additional optional equipment: tent, camp stove, lantern, cooking pots, ice chest, large drinking water container, towels, and warm clothing

You should also keep plenty of food and drinking water stored in your home. During shallow flooding, some homes may be cut off; if you are caught, it might take time until rescue crews arrive. If this should occur, you will need plenty of supplies on hand. It is important to replace water and any food subject to spoilage twice a year. To make it easier to remember, schedule checks on New Year's Day and the Fourth of July.

List #2 Important Documents

It's also important that insurance policies and other important documents be kept where they will be safe from flood water damage. A safe deposit box, in a neighbor's home or other location on high ground, will ensure their safety. Don't forget that banks, too, can be flooded, so safety deposit boxes in these buildings are less than ideal for document storage. The most important papers include:

- Will
- Insurance policies
- Contracts
- Deeds
- Stocks
- Bonds
- Passports

- Birth certificates
- Social security cards
- Immunization records
- Bank account numbers
- Credit card numbers
- Important phone numbers for friends, relatives, family doctor, and so on.

List #3 Things Needed *After* the Flood

When it is time to go back to your home after the flood is over, you will need some important items to begin recovering. These should be gathered and stored ahead of time because there is very little hope of finding them in a flooded household. If flood water is not expected to reach the second floor or attic, keep these supplies there. You can also put them in your car or at another site on high ground. Chances are most local stores will be out of them almost immediately, although relief agencies may supply some but not all to flood victims. Many of these items may already be included in your survival kit:

- Flashlight
- First aid kit
- Battery-operated radio
- Waterproof boots or waders
- Safety clothing: hard hat and gloves
- Boots or shoes with hard soles
- Dust mask
- Camera or video camera to record damage
- Tools: crowbar, hammer, saw, pliers, crescent wrench, screwdriver
- Drinking water
- Trash bags
- Cleaning supplies
- Fire extinguisher
- Strong tape (duct tape is ideal)
- Plastic sheeting
- Liquid chlorine bleach
- Plastic bucket with a tight lid
- Aluminum foil, paper, pencils, needle and thread
- A wooden stick for turning things over, scaring away snakes and small animals, and moving electrical wires

WHEN THE FLOOD COMES

The most important item during flooding is your portable radio because it is the lifeline that informs you of warnings, cresting, and the weather forecast. Shallow flooding may not be enough to cause evacuation, but, depending on the status of the flood water height, you may be forced to wait it out at home. In order to be prepared for this, fill bathtubs, sinks, and jugs with clean drinking water if you are on a municipal system. If your water comes from a domestic well, be sure to stockpile water *before* the wellhead is inundated to avoid contamination.

There are a few other last-minute things you can do to help your house and belongings to survive the flood. Board up the windows to protect them from the impact of debris floating by in the water; otherwise, they can break suddenly, sending glass fragments into the house. This reduces the chance of anyone inside's being cut by broken glass. Bring outdoor possessions inside, such as lawn furniture, garbage cans, tools, and signs, so they are not swept away.

If the water threatens to enter the first floor, move your emergency equipment to the second story, if there is one, or onto the roof. Many homes built in flood-ravaged areas have a trap door onto the roof because it can be very dangerous getting up there from a window. On the roof, stay where you will be visible to rescue workers. **Never try to wade or swim to safety!** Even 6 inches of fast-moving water can knock you off your feet.

Many floods have more than one crest, and the tendency is to go back into an inundated neighborhood as soon as the water level seems to be receding. Do not go back home before the local emergency broadcasts say it is safe.

Unexpected Health Hazards
Flood water can be very dangerous to your health, a fact many fail to realize. This water is not like that of a pond or lake—it is transient and covers a lot of ground, flowing across landfills, cemeteries, livestock enclosures, sewer plants, and a host of other unsavory sites. Most underground sewer systems back up into homes; septic leach lines may float up and out of the ground. Wherever the water travels, it picks up virtually anything, though we pay far more attention to large objects that cause serious damage. But it's not these that present the worst threat—it's the microscopic organisms. Harmful bacteria and toxic chemicals mix into the water, and although they are diluted, the threat of contamination is still very real. Historically, disease follows floods, such as those of nineteenth-century New Orleans, where epidemics of cholera were rampant after waters receded. This is because cholera is just one of many serious diseases infecting humans through the water supply.

When flood water enters a domestic well, it will contaminate the water and make it unsafe to drink. One thing you can do to lessen this problem is to duct-tape plastic around the cap to your well, which helps but does not eliminate the potential for contamination. The dangers also apply to public water supplies, treatment facilities, and pumping stations, which renders their water equally unfit for human consumption. This is the reason why there is such a paradox following flooding: Everywhere there is water, yet we must bring a potable supply in with tank trucks to thirsty survivors.

Flood water presents a serious hazard to pregnant women, who are at great risk of picking up dangerous bacteria and disease organisms. They should be evacuated immediately and return only when cleanup is completed. There is also a risk to small children because they are so quick to put their fingers and foreign objects in their mouths. Walking, wading, or swimming in flood water is not safe because every cut, scrape, or body orifice becomes an inroad for bacteria and toxic chemicals, which can result in serious infection. Virtually every surface and absorbent material may also contain harmful organisms. Therefore, personal hygiene is absolutely essential to keep all flood survivors

ELECTRICAL SAFETY

Tip #1 Many people feel it is important to turn off the electricity to the house before they evacuate. This can be **VERY DANGEROUS** and not worth the risk of electrocution if there is water anywhere near the house. Never touch any electrical equipment unless it is in a dry area and you are standing on a piece of dry wood while wearing rubber gloves and rubber-soled boots or shoes. Even with these precautions, it is better to leave the power on when you evacuate.

Tip #2 It is just as important to be aware of electricity after you return to your home. Few realize appliances contain capacitors that hold electrical current even after the unit has been unplugged. Beware of handling such equipment when standing in water or on wet ground. When you return to the house after the flood, the local utility company may have shut down the power, but you must still be sure to turn off all switches, including the main breaker, anyway. If the power comes back on unexpectedly, you could be at serious risk if standing in water or on a wet floor or if you or someone else is working on exposed wiring. **However, if you have to step in water to reach the electric box, do not attempt to touch it. Call an electrician. Do not assume that just because the electrical meter has been removed, the power is cut.**

Tip #3 Portable generators can be helpful during floods for power if electrical lines are down. Follow these guidelines for safe operation: Connect appliances one at a time. Use this and all other small gas engines outdoors, to avoid breathing dangerous carbon monoxide fumes. It's best not to use extension cords, but if unavoidable, check them frequently. If there is a chance of overloading, the cord will become hot and should be immediately unplugged.

Tip #4 During a flood or a hurricane there can be tremendous damage; often power lines are undermined and fall into the streets. Lines connecting buildings may also be cut. Electrical current can travel through flood waters, and many deaths are attributed to outdoor lines down in flooded areas. Report any such damage immediately to your utility company.

Therefore, personal hygiene is absolutely essential to keep all flood survivors and relief workers as healthy as possible.

The Red Cross suggests you following these guidelines during and after flood events:

1. Wash your hands with soap and water thoroughly and often. Preferably use an antibacterial soap. Be sure to clean under your fingernails.
2. Wash your hands and arms thoroughly before preparation of food and eating.
3. Smokers risk contamination with each cigarette; since smoking can be such an unconscious habit, they often forget to wash.
4. Nail biters beware, as this is also so automatic. Few stop to think, particularly under the stress of a natural disaster, which may increase the tendency for this habit.
5. If there are any animal carcasses in or around your house, call the health department for instructions before removing them.

A Case of Looters

In the 1986 flood of the Yuba River in California, three young men chose to remain behind to loot the undefended homes after the neighborhood had evacuated. They hid in their house and waited until dark, but discovered the water rising far faster than they expected, forcing them into the attic. What they hadn't counted on was that vermin for miles around were also searching for a dry place to spend the night. In horror the men remained in that attic, battling hordes of insects, rodents, and other wildlife, while the bone-chilling sounds of trapped animals filled the night. Needless to say, they practically kissed the police rescue team arriving at dawn, permanently curing the young men's lust for looting.

AFTER THE FLOOD

It can be emotionally devastating to return to a flood-damaged home, and the American Red Cross strongly suggests that victims remain conscious of their stress levels. Often the strain can tear apart families as poor food, lack of rest, and a grueling cleanup effort becomes overwhelming. If you feel depressed or your children are experiencing unusual problems such as bed-wetting, thumb-sucking, or clinging-behavior, seek professional

Mobile homes can suffer irreparable damage because most are not secured to a permanent foundation. Residents can lose everything even in very mild flooding and should take extra precautions to be sure their valuables are safe before the waters rise. (California Department of Water Resources)

help. After the flooding of 1994, the rate of teen suicide rose dramatically in Dade County, Florida. Take comfort in the fact that, with so many others sharing these same problems, special outreach and crisis counseling programs are organized by the Red Cross to help manage the emotional aftermath of disaster.

Buildings that have been flooded can be very dangerous: Ceilings can fall in, floors give way, and an entire structure can collapse with the weight of someone stepping inside. As a general rule, if there's standing water next to the outside walls of the house, don't enter; it's hard to tell whether it's structurally sound. Walk around the outside and look for loose power lines and signs or smells of gas leaks. Outdoor propane tanks tend to float and break away in floods, so these should be closely inspected. Propane will pool close to the ground and can be far more hazardous than natural gas, which is lighter and dissipates. **Do not smoke or use candles, gas lanterns, camp stoves, or any other open flame in or around the house until it has been inspected.** It's wise to ask an inspector or contractor to check everything out before you go inside. In fact, inspections are mandatory in many communities.

≣≣

> For detailed instructions on rehabilitating a flood-damaged home, contact the nearest FEMA office or the American Red Cross and obtain their free book *Repairing Your Flooded Home* (ARC 4477). It details in an easy-to-follow step-by-step format exactly what it takes to make most repairs, from restoring utilities to cleanup, and obtaining financial assistance. It is particularly helpful in explaining what is required to dry out and repair interior portions of the building.

≣≣

Flood waters damage a house in many different ways, and evidence of problems can be hidden within walls and beneath floors. Unless you are skilled in building trades, much of the repair work should be done by professionals, if possible. Silt buildup in nooks and crannies, if not removed right away, will linger indefinitely, harboring bacteria and fungi, which can cause all sorts of problems later on. Mildew and musty smells will sometimes linger for years if a home is not rehabilitated properly.

Landscape and Sprinklers

Just as the house must be completely cleaned up to remove the remains of contaminated water, the landscape, too, should be given a careful bath with the garden hose. Remove any new deposits of soil, and add earth where depressions have been created by scouring. If the lawn is covered with mud thicker than an inch deep, it may be much easier to simply plant a new lawn on top. If toxic materials were carried in the flood water, you may find that some plants

REVIVING YOUR HOUSEHOLD WATER SUPPLY
AFTER A FLOOD

BOIL ORDER When there is widespread contamination of the water supply, the authorities may issue an official boil order until the potable supply is restored. Although this can be time consuming, the threat of disease and infection should be taken seriously. You can use untreated water for flushing the toilet only. All water used for drinking, cooking, laundry, and washing dishes should be boiled according to this process:

1. Fill a large pot with tap water.
2. Strain the water through cheesecloth, a bed sheet, a coffee filter, or another clean, porous material to remove the solids.
3. Bring the water to a rolling boil, and keep it boiling for at least 10 minutes.
4. Pour the water back and forth between two pots to help it cool and add air, which makes it taste better.
5. Let the water cool, then add 8 drops of liquid chlorine bleach for each gallon of water. Let it stand for a half-hour; if it appears clear and there is a slight odor of chlorine, it is ready to use. If you don't smell chlorine and the water remains cloudy, add another 8 drops of bleach and let it stand an additional half-hour. If it still doesn't smell like chlorine, *do not use it* for drinking or cooking. Clorox or Purex brand bleach is fine to use, but avoid any brand that contains more than 5.25% sodium hypochlorite. Avoid scented bleach, as it influences water taste.

PRIVATE WELL Private domestic wells are frequently contaminated by flood water. Very shallow wells that draw off groundwater just below the surface may be subjected to long-term contamination. Fortunately, most wells draw from aquifers far beneath any effects of flooding. However, wells are usually contaminated when the wellhead becomes submerged and the flood water seeps in through the cap. Taping plastic over the wellhead does help reduce but not eliminate the problem. Contaminants can also enter through other openings, such as faucets and toilet tanks.

Many cities and counties have regulations about testing and decontaminating domestic wells after flooding. The local health department will provide information about testing your water and perhaps add to the following well-purification steps in areas where aquifer water quality is variable:

1. Open all the faucets inside and outside the house and let them run at least 15 minutes or until the well pressure drops. Turn off all the faucets.
2. Pour 1 quart of liquid chlorine bleach into the well and let it sit for at least 4 hours.
3. Then open all the faucets again, and let them run until the water at each one smells of chlorine.
4. Turn them off again and let the water sit in the pipes for 2 to 4 hours.
5. Open all the faucets again, and run them until you can no longer smell or taste chlorine.

had died anyway from contact; sometimes this is the result of an abundance of salt from coastal tidal surges. Refer to chapter 8 for detailed information on resurrecting the landscape after flooding.

If you have an underground sprinkler system, it can be damaged, buried, exposed, or clogged up by the flood. Most lines of a sprinkler system are not under constant pressure; they fill only when the valve is open and operating. Because they were empty and provided no resistance when the flood occurred, sediment would tend to work into and fill the system through the heads, unless they are the type with antisiphon mechanisms. When a system is under water, there is more pressure outside (water) than inside (air), and water naturally seeks and enters anywhere it can, typically through the heads.

If your yard is likely to flood again in the future, it's worth the cost of replacing existing heads with others more resistant to flood problems. A check valve allows water to flow in only one direction. Larger check valves are used on sewer lines in flood-prone areas to prevent sewage from backing up into houses while not blocking outflow. Sprinkler heads made with antisiphon or check valves were originally designed to prevent lawn chemicals from being sucked back into the city water supply after the water is shut off. They are also ideal heads for flood-prone lawn and planting areas. Although more expensive, they cut way down on damage and recovery time after even mild flooding.

The first step in restoring the sprinklers is to fill in wherever scouring has exposed the pipe. Then remove silt that has buried or mounded up around each head. If there has been a substantial overall rise in soil level or if heads have settled or are leaning, you may have to reset every head to restore proper coverage of the new surface. As long as the system is intact, you can remove and clean out every head, then replace them. Flush the lines by removing the head or heads farthest from the valve, so that any debris sitting in the pipes will be blown out at one or two points. Sometimes this takes a few tries because sprinklers can get clogged up again during the flushing process.

7
FUTURE FLOODING, FLOODPROOFING, AND DRAINAGE

Flood events are here to stay and are likely to increase for a variety of reasons. The floods of 1993 in the Mississippi watershed and those in the southeastern states, where a 500-year storm took everyone by surprise, both illustrate how unusual weather and rainfall totals can be deadly. Other factors already covered include increased runoff from development, with each new home or parking lot or freeway generating proportionately more runoff, which must be carried through our drainage systems. Decades of sediment deposits in storm drains, open ditches, behind dams, and at hydroelectric plants combine to decrease water-holding capacity and the effectiveness of all flood control structures.

Homes located this close to a waterway are vulnerable to flooding. Flood proofing is the only real means of long-term protection. (California Department of Water Resources)

For example, take a river that has been dammed to create a reservoir for a community. The river still flows, but now it must travel through the spillway instead of in a channel. When there is a lot of rainfall or spring runoff racing down the watershed, its velocity slows when it reaches the reservoir, and the sediment drops out. Most impoundments such as this were designed to hold a certain amount of sediment and still function properly, but if for some unexpected reason the amount is greater than the engineering calculations allowed for, then the reservoir will fill more rapidly. Each season the total sediment in the reservoir becomes a bit deeper and displaces a proportionate amount of water. Over time such action adds up to a loss of a sizable volume of holding capacity, as happens with many of our flood control and other water projects. What this means in terms of flooding is that more water is being forced through our rivers and streams each year.

A second problem relates to levees, which line both banks of most of our major rivers. There has been sediment accumulating in these constrained river channels, some already a century old. With walls of earth to prevent the flood water from spreading out, all the silt becomes concentrated in the channel to abnormal depth. Engineers grapple with this dilemma because reduction in channel volume means the levees must be built progressively higher to contain the 100-year storm flows. Not only that, but the land outside the levees may have been drained, and land subsidence may have caused an actual fall in elevation.

≡≡≡≡≡≡≡≡≡≡≡≡≡≡≡≡≡≡≡≡≡≡≡≡≡≡≡≡≡≡≡≡

Dredging the sediment out of our rivers is one solution, but it presents an awesome task. There are thousands of miles of rivers large and small in many different states and watersheds, each with its own set of constraints. Dredging is now complicated by environmental groups who feel any alteration to waterways, even for their own good, is too damaging to the ecology of rivers. In addition, funding for many large-scale flood works projects is dwindling.

≡≡≡≡≡≡≡≡≡≡≡≡≡≡≡≡≡≡≡≡≡≡≡≡≡≡≡≡≡≡≡≡

If you combine all the factors of weather, increased runoff, reduced reservoir capacity, and elevated river beds, there is little doubt we are bound to see even more flood problems in lowlands of America. Armed with this knowledge, it's easier to see why the Corps of Engineers is placing greater emphasis on bypasses and overflow wetlands as new flood control methods in their plans. If you are having problems with flooding now, it will gradually worsen over time. This inevitable and growing problem demands that city planners avoid placing new development within the 100-year flood plain. Unfortunately, this is some of the most valuable real estate for high-end waterfront homes and agriculture. The Corps also strongly suggests that anyone already living in a flood plain consider floodproofing in order to reduce flood insurance costs and increase the ability to ride out future floods reasonably unscathed.

FLOODPROOFING EXISTING AND NEW HOMES

Because most cities in America are located along rivers, there are a tremendous number of homes that should be floodproofed now or in the near future. Many people who

Moving a house to high ground as a method of floodproofing. (US Army Corps of Engineers, National Floodproofing Committee)

The Sacramento Governor's Mansion was built when the city still experienced frequent flooding. This house was constructed on top of a raised pad with the main floor a full story above that. Now obscured by lattice, the ground floor had many windows that were designed to allow water to flow through and thus reduce the pressure on foundations.

have been badly hurt by floods choose to move. Yet it is simply unrealistic to abandon entire neighborhoods and force residents to move to higher ground. Those emotionally attached to their community, or to the graceful river that has offered its beauty, cannot bear the thought of relocating, even with the knowledge that flooding will occur again.

The Army Corps of Engineers has developed a number of very successful techniques for floodproofing homes. The choice of which technique is best for you depends on the depth, velocity, frequency, and duration of flooding. Communities participating in the National Flood Insurance Program have already been studied to determine how flood losses can best be reduced by floodproofing. The NFIP provides financial assistance, lower premiums, and other incentives to homeowners who implement floodproofing of sites or buildings. It must be said that floods, as with other "acts of God," can be unpredictable; unexpectedly high flows or other anomalies can render even the best floodproofing program useless.

Sacramento, California, is a flood plain city, located at the confluence of the Sacramento and American Rivers. Since it was first settled by John Sutter in the early nineteenth century, the entire area has been subjected to periodic flooding, which is why Sutter built his fort on the only knoll in that part of the valley. Victorian homes built in Sacramento always placed the main floor on the second story. Old reports of Sacramento floods illustrate that these elevated homes were the only places for miles around where there was a chance of surviving the floods.

Sacramento old-timers tell us that ground floors usually had tall glass windows on every side for a reason. The forces of flowing water can be extreme when exerted against a stationary object in the stream. When the rivers of Sacramento flooded, these tall homes bore the brunt of water and debris floating in the water as well. The pressure quickly broke out the ground floor windows, which allowed the water to flow *through* the house and reduce the overall strain on the building. The goal was to keep the house standing as a haven for victims because there was no other high ground close by. In many respects these old homes implemented many of the floodproofing concepts used today.

Another side of the Governor's Mansion that clearly shows both the raised earth pad and the ground floor windows.

The ideal time to floodproof a house is right after a flood because so much, particularly the interior, has already been damaged. Making changes while doing these repairs becomes a "two birds with one stone" activity. However, if the house has been substantially damaged, you may find the cost of flood-proofing too high compared to the assessed value of the house before the flood. Floodproofing also has the psychological effect of providing assurance that the next battle with high water will not be so devastating to either the home or its contents. If you decide to sell sometime in the future, a floodproofed home will be far more valuable on the resale market.

Selecting the best floodproofing method for your house should be a deci-sion between you and an experienced local professional. Licensed architects, civil engineers, or general contractors who understand floodproofing technol-ogy are best suited to the task. They are guided by criteria developed by FEMA and the Army Corps of Engineers, as described in detail in many of their excel-lent floodproofing manuals. These publications tend to be geared toward the professional, but the photos and information are still helpful in illustrating how these methods look on actual floodproofed homes. You can obtain the fol-lowing titles from the nearest US Army Corps of Engineers office, FEMA, or through the NFIP: *Retrofitting Flood-Prone Residential Structures* (FEMA 114), *Flood Proofing Systems & Techniques, Elevated Residential Structures* (FEMA 54)

There are five methods of floodproofing used either in new construction or when retrofitting an existing home. Each has its pros and cons, which will ultimately determine which is best for your flood conditions, budget, site, and climate.

1. Elevation

Elevation is simply raising the first floor of a house so that it is located above the BFE indicated for that site. There are many different ways to support the elevated structure, and choices are dictated by local conditions. Elevation puts virtually all the living space of a house above the flood waters and thus protects both the structure and its contents. The material and structure below the BFE must be constructed so that during a flood the house won't float, collapse, or move around.

Many homes are ideal candidates for elevation, but certain building types make the job much more expensive and costly, sometimes eliminating elevation as a floodproofing option altogether. Houses over basements can be complicated: Utilities that are an integral part of the basement must be disconnected and elevated above the BFE. Some basements are incapable of sustaining the added loading forces of an elevated building, and extensive structural changes may be required. Houses without crawl space provide no access for workmen. To make room for the new foundations, large trenches must be excavated around and under the house for inserting the support beams needed to jack up the house. Houses built on concrete slabs are even more difficult because the utilities and foundation have been inserted into a single pad. To separate them is nearly impossible. Buildings constructed with such exterior materials as veneer brick or stucco suffer cracking and other problems under the strain of movement, particularly if they are multistory.

Below are five methods of elevating a house and the flood criteria that determine whether or not they can be used. For more information, contact your local building department.

1. **EXTENDED FOUNDATION WALLS** This uses your existing foundation and builds upon it to raise the first floor above the BFE.
   Flood criteria: Moderate depth, slow velocity.
2. **ELEVATION ON PIERS** Homes originally built on pier block

This home design incorporated a double staircase to reach the second floor, which has been elevated above the BFE. (US Army Corps of Engineers, National Floodproofing Committee)

This home along the banks of a major river has been floodproofed by extending the foundation so that the main floor is above the BFE. Parking, one of the few allowable uses below the BFE, is located on the ground floor. (US Army Corps of Engineers, National Floodproofing Committee)

The same home during flooding with the main floor high and dry above the water. (US Army Corps of Engineers, National Floodproofing Committee)

This home design incorporated a double staircase to reach the second floor, which has been elevated above the BFE. (US Army Corps of Engineers, National Floodproofing Committee)

Outdoor utilities such as the air conditioner are vulnerable to flooding. If the house is elevated to above the BFE, it is important to also raise up utilities as well. This reduces damage and the possibility of floating debris slamming into the unit. Elevation of indoor utilities such as the furnace and hot water heater in basements is just as important as these are below grade. This pad is made of a concrete block core veneered with brick, which will not float away and can resist the erosive forces of wave action.

SOME IMPORTANT TERMS AND BFE REQUIREMENTS

BFE: BASE FLOOD ELEVATION This is the elevation of the 100-year flood limit, as shown on the Flood Insurance Rate Maps. Most regulations stipulate the top of a building's lowest floor (including the basement) be elevated to or above the BFE.

A ZONE: SPECIAL FLOOD HAZARD AREA Any home or site located inside the 100-year flood plain

VERY SHALLOW FLOODING 1 foot or less in depth

SHALLOW FLOODING 1 to 3 feet in depth

MODERATE FLOODING 3 to 6 feet in depth

DEEP FLOODING 6 feet or more in depth

SLOW-MOVING FLOOD WATER Flowing at less than 3 feet per second

MODERATELY MOVING FLOOD WATER Flowing from 3 to 5 feet per second

FAST-MOVING FLOOD WATER Flowing at over 5 feet per second

YOU *CANNOT* LOCATE ANY OF THE FOLLOWING BELOW THE BFE:

- Basement
- Furnace
- Heatpump
- Hot water heater
- Air conditioner
- Washer
- Dryer
- Refrigerator/freezer
- Elevator
- Electrical panel
- Junction box

Living spaces, such as bedrooms, bath, kitchen, dining, living room, family room, or recreation room

YOU *MAY* LOCATE THESE BELOW THE BFE:

Vehicular parking, limited storage, and building access, e.g., stairs.

foundations or old homes with foundations that adapt to piers.
Flood criteria: Shallow depth, slow to moderate velocity.

3. **ELEVATION ON POSTS OR COLUMNS** The home is set upon a series of wood, steel, or concrete posts that have been set in concrete and connected with a bracing system.
Flood criteria: Shallow to moderate depth, slow to moderate velocity.

4. **ELEVATION ON PILINGS** Wood pilings are pounded deep into the earth for stability in coastal conditions where storm surges can be both deep and powerful, or where soil conditions are poor.

Flood criteria: Deep flooding, high velocity.
5. **ELEVATION ON FILL** Building pad is constructed of elevated compacted soil. This is a frequent means of getting above the BFE in newly constructed homesites, but is not well suited to retrofitting.
Flood criteria: Shallow depth, low velocity.

Houses can be moved in pieces. Here, a garage is being moved. (US Army Corps of Engineers, National Floodproofing Committee)

2. Relocation

In some areas simply moving a house to higher ground presents the only viable option, and moving also assures you permanent relief from future flooding. This is ideal for people who own a large piece of land with a suitable alternate site at a higher elevation. When considering this option, keep in mind the discussion at the opening of this chapter on sediment buildup and the reduced capacities of rivers and other water bodies: Be sure the new site is far enough above the BFE to allow for gradual increases in flood levels.

3. Levees and Berms

Sometimes it's possible to protect a home with miniature levees, just as entire towns are protected by levee systems. Levees should be used only

Entire houses can be relocated out of the hazard area, and in this case many homes are moving at the same time. When homes are moved there are many permits and obstructions in the roadway to contend with, and it is sometimes more cost effective to obtain clearances all at once than one at a time. (US Army Corps of Engineers, National Floodproofing Committee)

on sites experiencing shallow and moderate flood depths and low velocity, since earth of any kind is subjected to the effects of erosion when in contact with moving water. Levees are inexpensive if you have a large piece of property that contains a suitable **borrow area** from which you can excavate enough fill to create the berms. A borrow area can be vegetated and filled with water for an attractive pond or wetland habitat once you're through. If you don't have a borrow site, then the levee costs more because you must obtain fill and have it hauled in by truck. Perhaps one of the nicest benefits to this method is that levees can be disguised with landscape plants to be less apparent.

Homes can be surrounded by their own small levee where the BFE is low enough. This example shows how the driveway and other access points must pass over the levee to reach the house. (US Army Corps of Engineers, National Floodproofing Committee)

Floodwalls can be some of the most attractive ways of floodproofing a house. When the wall is located further away from the building it is not so obvious, and there are more options for making creative outdoor spaces and blending the wall into the landscape. The more area protected inside the floodwall, the less damage to patios and gardens, and the easier it will be to dig out. (US Army Corps of Engineers, National Floodproofing Committee)

The down side is that levees must be well maintained and repaired now and then; they often go neglected until flood water finds its way into irregularities or eroded pockets. It is essential that you inspect for signs of erosion, settlement, or cracking. Any soil-holding vegetation on the levee must be replanted if a portion of it dies. The height of the levee will be determined by

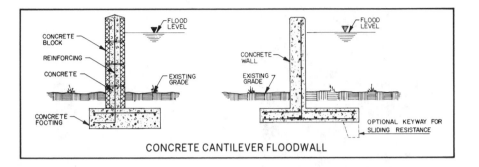

CONCRETE CANTILEVER FLOODWALL

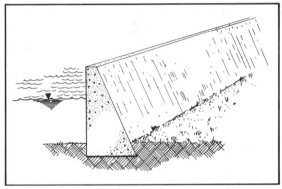

A floodwall must be able to sustain the pressure of water, which can be far greater than most people realize. In fact, a floodwall is nearly identical to a retaining wall, which usually requires special design if it is to do the job without failure. In order for a floodwall to remain upright under the weight and forces of flowing water filled with debris, there must be a very large "cantilever" footing. Gravity floodwalls are slightly different in that they do not require such a large footing, but the wall itself must be far more massive to sustain the loads. With the mass of a gravity wall or the large footing of a floodwall, the amount of material and steel reinforcement makes them very expensive to build. (US Army Corps of Engineers, National Floodproofing Committee)

flood data, and there should always be additional **freeboard**, which provides a margin of safety against overtopping if flood levels are higher than expected. Levees less than 3 feet in height should have 1 foot of freeboard. For those any taller, a freeboard of 3 feet is recommended.

On-site drainage can also be a problem because the levee has isolated your home and immediate yard from the surrounding watershed. If water builds up inside the levee, you may need to pump it out or provide some other kind of mechanical drainage device. An on-site borrow area may be graded out softly to serve as a detention basin to collect drainage from the site and hold it there until it is pumped over the levee. There is also the need to route walks and driveways over the levee in order to connect the house with the street.

A floodwall must have openings to enter the house, and these must be sealed if the wall is to be effective. This means closing the front entry and a driveway if the garage is part of the house. These closures must be water-tight and very strong, so they are most often made out of heavy gauge steel as the one shown here. The major drawback of the floodwall systems is that some-one must manually seal the closures, and if no one is available the home will be flooded. (US Army Corps of Engineers, National Floodproofing Committee)

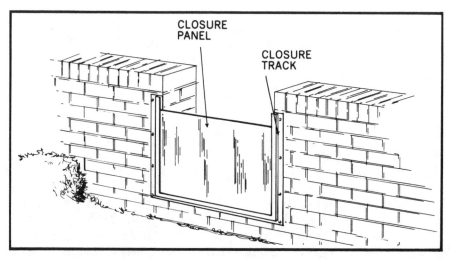

Detail of how a floodwall closure is attached to the wall itself. (US Army Corps of Engineers, National Floodproofing Committee)

This aerial view shows a flooded home well protected by the floodwall that surrounds the dwelling. (US Army Corps of Engineers, National Floodproofing Committee)

The creation of a berm or levee system always has an impact on drainage or flows, and is often prohibited by local zoning laws. This is because you are creating a permanent element in the flood plain that directs the flow of water around it. This may flood neighboring property or have other effects on surrounding drainage systems. You may be required to obtain a permit before you can begin work on the levee. For all these reasons, it is worth the expense of hiring a civil engineer to design your levee system, work out the drainage complications and figure out the best way to get autos in and out.

Flood criteria: Shallow to moderate depth, slow velocity.

4. Floodwalls

A floodwall acts in much the same way as a levee by presenting a physical barrier between your house and flood water. Floodwalls are more expensive than levees because they are typically made of steel-reinforced concrete, with oversized footings for stability under the awesome weight of high water. You would be surprised how much concrete is required to construct just 1 linear foot of wall, because nearly half of it is underground when constructed with a cantilevered footing. Walls can also be constructed of masonry block, but this material can only be used on the aboveground portions, while the footing must still be made of poured concrete.

Gravity floodwalls require a similar amount of concrete, but the design utilizes the mass of the wall for strength rather than a large footing. A gravity wall allows you to landscape on both sides of the wall, whereas a cantilever footing gets in the way on one side.

Floodwalls can be veneered with attractive used brick which ties in well with the house. A barrier, or "closure," will be required to seal this area where the driveway accesses the garage. (US Army Corps of Engineers, National Floodproofing Committee)

Floodwalls are more attractive when the concrete core is veneered with brick or stone. Masonry block can also be purchased with a "slump," split-face, or scored side, which creates an attractive finish texture. Far cheaper than veneer or decorative masonry block is a good landscape of vines and shrubs, which can eliminate a good portion of a plain floodwall from view. Flood criteria: Low to moderate depth, slow to moderate velocity.

5. Sealants or Dry Floodproofing

This method seals the outer walls of the house itself as barriers to the flood water, but the house must be structurally capable of withstanding the tremendous pressure of moving water. This pressure is compounded by the potential impact loads of objects slamming against the building. For this reason dry floodproofing is limited to brick veneer and masonry construction that is in *good structural condition.*

This tall brick floodwall has a core of either concrete block or poured concrete. It creates a sheltered courtyard inside which can become an attractive outdoor living space. (US Army Corps of Engineers, National Floodproofing Committee)

The most common way to permanently seal the house is to add a veneer of brick on top of the existing wall, with layers of waterproofing material sandwiched in between. This additional veneer layer also strengthens the house against impact loads.

Wrapping a house is a more temporary, emergency form of sealing. It is simply wrapping the lower part of the house in 6-mil polyethylene plastic. Material made for this purpose is typically 8 feet wide, which allows for good anchorage in the soil at the bottom of the wall, while the top edge is duct-taped to the wall. The plastic must always be laid against a solid surface because it does not have enough strength to hold off the pressure of water; it simply prevents its passing through. Beware around doorways, vents, and other breaks in the building wall, which do not normally offer sufficient support.

There is also the potential for the house to float if it experiences unusually deep flooding. A sealed house can suffer buoyancy-related damage in three ways.

1. Wood-framed houses will *float* at water depths of less than 3 feet above the first floor.
2. Those of brick or masonry built on a concrete slab may suffer *buckling* of the slab when water is 3 feet deep.
3. Homes subjected to the pressure of water in the surrounding soil can suffer basement damage when the slab floor of the basement *floats or buckles* at water depths 4 feet above the basement floor.

Flood criteria: Shallow depth, very low velocity.

Floodwalls can be constructed of split face concrete block for a rough decorative texture or be veneered with stone. (US Army Corps of Engineers, National Floodproofing Committee)

Floodwalls create a barrier separating the house from the surrounding land. During rainy weather runoff from the house and spaces inside the floodwall will collect with nowhere to go. This is also a problem with levee protections. A sump pump is essential if the water is to be pumped over the wall or levee and prevent standing water inside where it can damage the house. (US Army Corps of Engineers, National Floodproofing Committee)

DRAINAGE IN WET SOILS

Two of the most difficult dilemmas facing a homeowner are drainage and how to make plants grow in wet soil. After flooding, the original drainage methods and systems usually fail to work due to changes in grades, clogging of inlets and pipes, or debris in open channels. Most homesites in flood plains lie on flat ground with virtually no slope at all, which makes it difficult to move water or make it drain away. This can be even more difficult in back yards where the water must drain around the house and out to the street curb. In critical situations it's well worth the expense of hiring a civil engineer to design a system for you.

There are a few simple drainage techniques used in landscaping that can be installed by just about anyone. The key is understanding your drainage problem and the factors involved. Ask yourself the following questions and see whether the answers will influence drainage around your home.

Is poor drainage a problem during some seasons or all year round? Poor drainage in the winter is less damaging because plants are dormant and do not need to obtain as much oxygen from the soil. Saturated soil or standing water during the summer months can be deadly to plants, which is often the case where thunderstorms cause widespread flooding in warm weather.

Is your soil dense clay, caliche, hardpan, or adobe? Dense soils are very slow to absorb water, but once saturated, virtually nothing will grow in them. Drainage problems can occur when irrigation water is applied faster than the soil can absorb it. Heavy clay will remain wet for a very long time and resist drying out unless an underground drainage system is installed.

This building has been sealed so that all parts below the BFE are waterproofed. This effectively protects the ground floor and eliminates damage to any utilities and improvements located there as well. (US Army Corps of Engineers, National Floodproofing Committee)

The doorway to this building can be sealed with a barrier if flooding is expected. (US Army Corps of Engineers, National Floodproofing Committee)

Does water flow into your yard from somewhere else? In many areas certain homesites suffer from drainage that originates in other places. For example, if a house is at the bottom of a long slope, the accumulative runoff from that slope pours straight down on this single homesite. No simple drainage system will accommodate such flows, making an off-site system to divert this runoff the most effective solution. Drainage problems can also occur when runoff from your next-door neighbor flows onto your lot. It is better to notify the neighbor of the problem than to try and manage the additional water yourself.

Is there a storm drain nearby? Homes in the suburbs or on flat land have nowhere to send their excess water. A storm drain fed by inlets along a curb line is the ideal place to which your lot should drain, but water cannot cross a sidewalk, driveway, or curb. It must be piped under the sidewalk and through the curb to prevent accidents and a hazard to foot traffic. If no storm drain is handy, there is often no choice but to create a gravel sump in a far corner of the yard, where water can collect underground and gradually soak into the surrounding soil. Although this is not ideal, it is relatively inexpensive.

Surface type	Maximum Slope	Minimum Slope
Driveway	5%	1%
Concrete walkway	5%	0.5%
Flagstone or brick paving	2%	1%
Lawn	3%	2%

A 1% slope = 1 foot vertical fall in 100 feet horizontal distance.

When professionals design sites, they establish certain gradients to ensure water flows where desired and with the minimum amount of contour grading. Here are some widely used gradients. Slopes are limited to a maximum percentage to keep flow velocity slow and reduce scouring. Minimum slope gradients ensure there is enough fall to make the water flow properly. Ideally, a greater slope than the minimum should be used, but on very flat land where there is no relief, the minimum is critical.

Basic Drainage Structures

You may have some of these devices installed at your home or nearby. It is essential that some be cleaned out frequently. For example, a drainage ditch allowed to become choked with weeds and grasses or garbage loses a very large percentage of its capacity. A documented case involving a sizeable ditch in Louisiana had a measured capacity just one-tenth of its original capacity only 2 years after it was excavated. The damage was caused by heavy growth of grasses and indigo. Uncontrolled brush and trees can reduce the

When flooding is shallow and only a few inches above grade, small floodwalls can be constructed that prevent the water from entering windows or doors. (US Army Corps of Engineers, National Floodproofing Committee)

A temporary barrier of waterproof plastic can be installed around a house if flooding is expected. This is a good method to use in less flood-prone areas, which may be vulnerable only to the 500-year flood. (US Army Corps of Engineers, National Floodproofing Committee)

capacity of any ditch to one-third to one-half of its proper carrying capacity in just 3 to 5 years.

The basic concept behind most drainage techniques is based on two truths:

1. **Water always flows out of an area of greater concentration into one of lesser concentration.** A good example is ditch drainage, where a trench dug in saturated soil creates an area with no water concentration. Immediately, water will flow out of both walls of the trench, thus draining the surrounding soil. If enough water collects in the ditch to fill it half full, then only the top half will continue to drain as before. The bottom half has reached equilibrium, where water concentration in the soil is equal to the water concentration in the bottom half of the trench.

2. **Water always flows downhill.** Design of drainage systems always begins with the elevation of the final destination of the water. From there the grades are worked back uphill until the entire system is engineered with proper flow line gradients and surface inlet elevations.

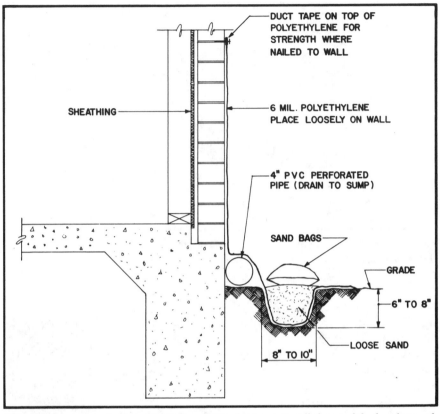

DUCT TAPE ON TOP OF
POLYETHYLENE FOR
STRENGTH WHERE
NAILED TO WALL

SHEATHING

6 MIL. POLYETHYLENE
PLACE LOOSELY ON WALL

4" PVC PERFORATED
PIPE (DRAIN TO SUMP)

SAND BAGS

GRADE

6" TO 8"

LOOSE SAND

8" TO 10"

This detail shows exactly how polyethylene plastic sheeting is installed around the foundation of a house to temporarily prevent water from entering during a flood. It is well anchored in the soil with a trench and the plastic is taped to the wall above the expected water level. Any openings in the building wall, such as crawl space vents, must be reinforced because the plastic will tear if not properly supported. (US Army Corps of Engineers, National Floodproofing Committee)

If flooding occurs while ditches are in this condition, there is an increased chance it will overflow its banks and inundate nearby homesites. Therefore, drainage structures remain effective only when

1. they are properly designed with sufficient slope to guarantee flows,
2. vegetation is kept controlled in and around the structure, and
3. silt and sediment deposits are periodically removed to maintain capacity.

DITCH DRAINS AND SWALES A ditch drain is simply an open ditch which gathers water from the surface or upper layer of the soil to the same depth as the

Basement windows can be sealed against very shallow flood waters with low walls tied into the foundation. ((US Army Corps of Engineers, National Floodproofing Committee)

bottom of the trench. This is the method used by early American farmers to drain overly wet ground to render it productive cropland. The steeper the sides of the ditch, the less tendency there will be for vegetation to grow and the faster the water flows. Ditches can be in a V shape or a U shape, depending on what kind of equipment is used to dig them.

A ditch drain used in landscaping is called a **swale**. It is not so geometric in shape but graded out with soft curves and forms to blend more naturally with the surroundings. Soft slopes also allow grass or other types of ornamental plants to grow in and around the swale to reduce erosion.

Drainage ditches not properly maintained are destined to back up when needed most. Large obstructions tend to catch floating debris and may block the flow enough to cause widespread flooding upstream. (California Department of Water Resources)

Ditches and swales are often placed beside roads and driveways to collect and channel runoff from these surfaces. During heavy rainfall it is these ditches that overflow and inundate rural roadways. Being constructed only of earth, they will eventually deteriorate if weedy vegetation is allowed to grow unchecked. If there is sufficient erosion on the side walls, they can collapse, and the soil will block the flow line and cause back-up flooding. Many of these

116

USING THE DECISION MATRIX TO HELP CHOOSE THE BEST FLOODPROOFING METHOD

There are many factors to consider when choosing a floodproofing method for your house. FEMA and the Federal Insurance Administration have created a matrix that takes into consideration everything from flood type to site and building characteristics. Before using the matrix you should do some research to obtain the information needed to answer the questions. You should first know whether your house is built upon a raised foundation, an on-grade foundation (no crawl space), or a concrete slab. Study the local FIRMs (flood maps) to know the depth of flooding expected in your neighborhood, and consult with local emergency and flood control agencies for details regarding velocity, duration, debris loads, and soils.

To use the matrix, simply circle the yes or no of each column as it applies to you, as illustrated. For example, if your flood depth is rated "moderate" in the retrofitting factors column, then you would circle "yes" under each floodproofing method described at the top. When you've done the same for all ten factor categories, add up the number of "yes" answers in each vertical column and write the total in the blank at the bottom. The example of a completed matrix shows varying scores for each category. Those with a 10 prove to be the best choices for this homeowner.

ditches are channeled into culverts, which are the open drainpipes installed beneath roads and driveways. It is essential to keep all ditches and swales in good condition, and if necessary, gunite or cobble riprap should be installed to prevent erosion and collapse. If velocities are too rapid, which is often the reason for erosion, then checkdams may be required. However, it is wise to obtain advice from a civil engineer or local official before attempting a checkdam or other alterations of the ditch.

To reduce flooding, keep your ditches and swales in good condition. Pay particular attention to culverts, which can be blocked with debris, which would force water to overtop the roadway and wash it out. Headwalls, the reinforcement around the culvert, should be kept in good repair. After a flood be sure to clean out ditches and culverts right away to be sure the debris does not pose a health hazard. If there is a chance of further flooding in the near future, clean ditches and culverts will assure you of maximum drainage ability.

DECISION MATRIX

RETROFITTING FACTORS	ELEVATION ON FOUNDATION WALL (CHAPTER 3.5)	ELEVATION ON PIERS (CHAPTER 3.7)	ELEVATION ON POSTS OR COLUMNS (CHAPTER 3.8)	ELEVATION ON PILES (CHAPTER 3.9)	RELOCATION (CHAPTER 4)	LEVEES (CHAPTER 4)	FLOODWALLS (CHAPTER 6)	FLOODWALLS WITH CLOSURES (CHAPTER 7)	SEALANTS AND	CLOSURES (CHAPTER 8)
1. Flood Depth										
Shallow (less than 3 feet)	YES	YES	YES	YES	YES	YES	YES	YES	YES	YES
Moderate (3 to 6 feet)	YES	YES	YES	YES	YES	YES	YES	YES	NO	NO
Deep (greater than 6 feet)	YES	YES	YES	YES	YES	NO	NO	NO	NO	NO
2. Flood Velocity										
Slow (less than 3 fps)	YES	YES	YES	YES	YES	YES	YES	YES	YES	YES
Moderate (3 to 5 fps)	YES	YES	YES	YES	YES	YES	YES	YES	NO	NO
Fast (greater than 5 fps)	NO	NO	YES	YES	YES	NO	NO	NO	NO	NO
3. Flash Flood Potential										
Yes	NO	YES	YES	YES	YES	YES	YES	NO	NO	NO
No	YES	YES	YES	YES	YES	YES	YES	YES	YES	YES
4. Long Duration Flooding										
Yes	YES	YES	YES	YES	YES	NO	NO	NO	NO	NO
No	YES	YES	YES	YES	YES	YES	YES	YES	YES	YES
5. Debris/Ice Floe Potential										
Yes	NO	YES	YES	YES	YES	YES	YES	NO	NO	NO
No	YES	YES	YES	YES	YES	YES	YES	YES	YES	YES
6. Site Location										
Floodway or Coastal V-Zone	NO	YES	YES	YES	YES	NO	NO	NO	NO	NO
Riverine Floodplain	YES	YES	YES	YES	YES	YES	YES	YES	YES	YES
7. Soil Type										
Permeable	NO	YES	YES	YES	YES	NO	NO	NO	NO	NO
Impermeable	YES	YES	YES	YES	YES	YES	YES	YES	YES	YES
8. Building Foundation										
Slab on Grade	YES	YES	YES	NO	NO	YES	YES	YES	YES	YES
Crawl Space or Basement	YES	YES	YES	YES	YES	YES	YES	YES	YES	YES
9. Building Construction Type										
Concrete or Masonry	YES	YES	YES	NO	YES	YES	YES	YES	YES	YES
Wood	YES	YES	YES	YES	YES	YES	YES	YES	NO	NO
10. Building Condition										
Excellent to Good	YES	YES	YES	YES	YES	YES	YES	YES	YES	YES
Fair to Poor	NO	NO	NO	NO	NO	YES	YES	YES	NO	NO
TOTAL TIMES FEASIBLE										

KEY: USING THE RETROFITTING FACTORS, THE METHODS THAT COLLECT THE MOST FEASIBLE VOTES SHOULD BE EXAMINED IN DETAIL FOR RETROFITTING YOUR RESIDENTIAL STRUCTURE.

Blank Decision Matrix Retrofitting Methods of Flood Proofing.

Drainage of soil after flooding is critical, but clogged ditches will inhibit this drying-out process.

FRENCH DRAINS These underground drains function the same way as ditches: by drawing water out of the surrounding wet soil into a void. The void can be made with gravel or perforated pipe, which acts very much like leach lines in a septic system, only in reverse. The good thing about French drains is that they remain out of sight and are less likely to become choked with weeds.

DECISION MATRIX B

RETROFITTING FACTORS	Elevation on Foundation Wall (Chapter 3.5)	Elevation on Piers (Chapter 3.7)	Elevation on Posts or Columns (Chapter 3.8)	Elevation on Piles (Chapter 3.9)	Relocation (Chapter 4)	Levees (Chapter 4)	Floodwalls (Chapter 6)	Floodwalls with Closures (Chapter 7)	Sealants and	Closures (Chapter 8)
1. Flood Depth										
Shallow (less than 3 feet)	YES	YES	YES	YES	YES	YES	YES	YES	YES	YES
Moderate (3 to 6 feet)	YES	YES	YES	YES	YES	YES	YES	YES	YES	YES
Deep (greater than 6 feet)	YES	YES	YES	YES	YES	NO	NO	NO	NO	NO
2. Flood Velocity										
Slow (less than 3 fps)	YES	YES	YES	YES	YES	YES	YES	YES	YES	YES
Moderate (3 to 5 fps)	YES	YES	YES	YES	YES	YES	YES	YES	NO	NO
Fast (greater than 5 fps)	NO	NO	YES	YES	YES	NO	NO	NO	NO	NO
3. Flash Flood Potential										
Yes	NO	YES	YES	YES	YES	YES	YES	NO	NO	NO
No	YES	YES	YES	YES	YES	YES	YES	YES	YES	YES
4. Long Duration Flooding										
Yes	YES	YES	YES	YES	YES	NO	NO	NO	NO	NO
No	YES	YES	YES	YES	YES	YES	YES	YES	YES	YES
5. Debris/Ice Floe Potential										
Yes	NO	YES	YES	YES	YES	YES	YES	NO	NO	NO
No	YES	YES	YES	YES	YES	YES	YES	YES	YES	YES
6. Site Location										
Floodway or Coastal V-Zone	NO	YES	YES	YES	YES	NO	NO	NO	NO	NO
Riverine Floodplain	YES	YES	YES	YES	YES	YES	YES	YES	YES	YES
7. Soil Type										
Permeable	NO	YES	YES	YES	YES	NO	NO	NO	NO	NO
Impermeable	YES	YES	YES	YES	YES	YES	YES	YES	YES	YES
8. Building Foundation										
Slab on Grade	YES	YES	YES	NO	NO	YES	YES	YES	YES	YES
Crawl Space or Basement	YES	YES	YES	YES	YES	YES	YES	YES	YES	YES
9. Building Construction Type										
Concrete or Masonry	YES	YES	YES	NO	YES	YES	YES	YES	YES	YES
Wood	YES	YES	YES	YES	YES	YES	YES	YES	NO	NO
10. Building Condition										
Excellent to Good	YES	YES	YES	YES	YES	YES	YES	YES	YES	YES
Fair to Poor	NO	NO	NO	NO	NO	YES	YES	YES	NO	NO
TOTAL TIMES FEASIBLE	8	10	10	10	10	8	8	8	6	6

KEY: USING THE RETROFITTING FACTORS, THE METHODS THAT COLLECT THE MOST FEASIBLE VOTES SHOULD BE EXAMINED IN DETAIL FOR RETROFITTING YOUR RESIDENTIAL STRUCTURE.

Sample Completed Decision Matrix Retrofitting Methods of Flood Proofing

They can also be arranged in a variety of patterns to better drain large areas than surface ditches. However, over time soil filters into the gravel and eventually reduces its water-holding capacity. During flooding these drains are less effective because there is so much water and no place for it to go.

The oldest method of field drainage used by early American farmers involved burial of clay pipe called **drain tile**. Water in the surrounding soil would seep through the clay or through joints between segments. A modern

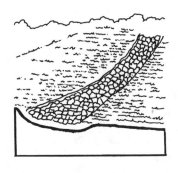

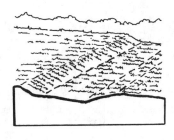

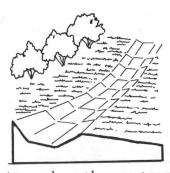

Drainage swales must have some type of soil stabilization if they are to remain in good condition and avoid erosion. Top: Swale is lined with rock cobble riprap which also helps reduce velocity. Center: Landscape swales may be located in lawns because the turf grass keeps the surface well stabilized. Bottom: In areas where excessive flows are expected, swales and ditches can be lined with concrete, usually gunite.

version replaces clay drain tile with perforated plastic pipe. The pipe is laid upon a bed of gravel in the bottom of a trench, then covered up with another layer of gravel. Rather than placing dirt right on top of the gravel, lay a strip of fiberglass insulation, roofing felt, or canvas upon the gravel, then replace the dirt. These coverings block dirt from falling down into the gravel and keeps the capacity of the drain intact for as long as possible.

SURFACE DRAINS In many urban areas, underground drainpipes gather and funnel water into the storm drain. Typically these pipes are 3 or 4 inches in diameter and are fed by catch basins, drop inlets, or surface drain grates. Drop inlets are designed to catch sediment traveling in the water by allowing it to settle out at a point where the debris can easily be removed by hand. Surface drains typically used in residential landscaping are either flat-topped or domed. Leaves, mulch, and even dirt can move with the runoff to accumulate over a flat-topped surface drain, blocking it entirely. If a domed cap is used, the debris collects around the edge. If the water becomes deep enough, however, it gets over this barrier and enters the drain lines.

The effectiveness of a surface drain can be limited if material collects in the underground lines, particularly if they were laid with a minimum degree of slope. More gradual slopes do not allow the water to reach a high enough velocity to dislodge the blockage. Well-designed systems provide clean-outs at critical locations so that the garden hose can be inserted to flush the lines. Piping can be made of rigid polystyrene because it is never under pressure. Another popular type is black plastic and corrugated to bend around corners, which eliminates the need for too many fittings.

DIVERSION DITCH A diversion ditch simply gathers runoff and diverts it somewhere else. Anyone familiar with tent camping knows it's best to dig a little trench around the uphill side of the tent. This is so that rainwater is diverted around the tent, keeping it dry. Diversion ditches can be used to help reduce runoff draining down the face of slopes. Unchecked, this condition leads to an overly wet toe of the slope and can even contribute to serious mudslides and embankment failure. Diversion ditches can be located to channel this runoff elsewhere, rather than allowing it to run straight down the whole face of the slope.

Whenever you install underground drainage devices, it is very important to be aware of what is growing on top of or around them. Trees and shrubs such as willows and other wetland plants have extensive fibrous roots that aggressively seek out water. They find a perfect home in French drains and sumps and enter perforated pipe through the holes. It's best to keep these plants away from drainage features; when that isn't possible, consider Typar biobarrier, a new product developed for urban street trees that tend to damage paving and utilities. Biobarrier consists of a thick sheet of plastic with round bumps all over the surface containing a slow-release herbicide. When tree roots contact the barrier, the herbicide kills the tips without hurting the plant. Lining biobarrier plastic in or around some of these drainage features makes sure they won't be invaded by water-hungry roots. It will extend the life of underground drains considerably. You can obtain this product through most garden centers, or ask at your local public works department for nearby suppliers.

In many subdivisions where extensive cut-and-fill building pads have been carved out of the earth, engineers design horizontal diversion ditches at regular intervals to collect water flowing down the slope and funnel it off to the side. On a cut slope, a diversion ditch can also be located above the cut line, so runoff from the natural hill above never reaches the bare cut. Emergency diversion ditches can be dug just before storms, or even during storms because that's when you're most likely to know exactly how the water flows. During sheet flooding these can be a good way to reduce impact on a homesite, but they are of little use in deeper water.

GRAVEL SUMPS For flatlanders there is always a problem with gradients. With no appreciable slope to the surface of the ground, it is nearly impossible to tie into storm drains and still ensure proper flow rates. This is also a big

Canals that carry irrigation water or runoff can become choked with vegetation, which greatly reduces their capacity.

dilemma for suburban and rural residents, who have no storm drains at all, and whose nearest ditch may be far away. Although it is not ideal, and even ineffective during flooding or where the water table is close to the surface, a **gravel sump** provides an option. This is simply a holding tank for water from surface or underground drainage systems. The water sits in the sump until it can gradually seep into the surrounding soil at its own rate. Most sumps are packed with gravel just like a vertical French drain, or they can be constructed with very large-diameter clay or perforated pipe buried in a deep hole on end. Gravel-packed sumps, the easiest to build, average about 24 inches in diameter, but this is not a rule—just a guideline. They can be larger or smaller as required. Be sure to cap off the gravel with roofing felt or fiberglass to prevent sifting of soil and filling of the sump.

Engineers use this method on a larger scale with a **drain field**, where a number of gravel sumps are clustered in the lowest point of the site to catch drainage and keep it below the surface of the soil. Drain fields are sometimes used in public parks, where large expanses of lawn make it difficult to use other drainage methods. Turf grasses grow well over drain fields since they don't have very deep roots, which would infiltrate the gravel and reduce capacity.

8
THE EFFECTS OF FLOODING ON SOIL AND PLANTS

P roblems accompanying flooding can have long-term impact on plants. Any plant going under fast-moving water will suffer some damage, but it is the invisible changes that can be most frustrating. Alteration of soil fertility, impossible drainage, and microscopic diseases frequently follow where land has been inundated. The early farmers of America's rich river bottoms forever battled these threats and often had no idea why their crops failed. For just as the infertile sand of the desert is reluctant to support plant life, wet soil is equally uncooperative.

The following definitions will assist you in better understanding the relationship of water to soil:

WATER TABLE The upper surface of groundwater; the level below which the soil is saturated with water

WATERLOGGED, SATURATED All voids in the soil filled with water

AEROBIC With air or oxygen

ANAEROBIC Without air or oxygen

SOIL DAMAGE
The single biggest impact on healthy soil inundated with flooding is saturation. Saturated soil can suffer the effects for a very long time because the balance of microorganisms, organic matter, and oxygen is altered.

Most people think that flooding is good for the soil, but this isn't always the case. Flood waters can lay down deposits of silt, which vary in fertility, but they can also leave gravel and sand. The real threat is from saturation of the soil and the length of time the soil is in that condition. Saturated soil becomes anaerobic, a state affecting future drainage, soil fertility, and a plant's ultimate survival. What makes this most difficult to both understand and rectify is that in most cases these changes are invisible.

Soil is alive. It contains different types of tiny microorganisms, such as fungi, algae, and bacteria, which contribute to soil fertility. Some function better under dry conditions, such as the fungi, which reproduce well in soil with normal oxygen content. On the other hand, algae, which we know thrive in stagnant pools of oxygen-depleted water, also thrive when a soil is saturated.

Under these conditions, algae and other anaerobic microorganisms may reproduce in great numbers. When flooding occurs in the warmer months, as it does in the Midwest and South, they can overpopulate the soil and fill every tiny space with offspring. This double whammy—no oxygen and too much algae—leaves the soil with very little drainage ability after the waters recede. As the algae dry out, the surface soil becomes glued into a single mass. Eventually, the fungi return and the soil will normalize, but in the meantime this dense layer restricts water percolation into the soil. This is much the same reaction sought by farmers trying to seal the bottom of a newly dug agricultural pond.

A constant exchange of gases occurs in healthy soil as a part of the decomposition of organic matter. This process is altered when the matter is denied oxygen from poor drainage or when covered with flood waters in warm climates. In colder climates, decomposition can slow or stop altogether in saturated soil. Peat bogs are thus formed by centuries of accumulating organic matter that does not decompose.

Normally, flooded or saturated soil becomes unstable, and gases such as carbon dioxide accumulate, their exit blocked by the surface covering of water or saturated soil. These toxic gases are prevented from venting into the atmosphere and thus accumulate to unhealthy levels in the soil.

The most obvious indicator of this condition is the unpleasant odor the soil releases when exposed to air. A common example of this can be found in potted houseplants that have been overwatered. When the plant is pulled out of the pot, the soil inside is black and smells rotten. This is the accumulation of gases finally being released. Air exchange is why some gardeners insist on using unfired clay pots instead of plastic ones. Clay is porous, so these gases will gradually filter through, not build up. While clay pots aren't efficient in terms of conserving water, which also filters out, they do help reduce the chances of overwatering.

In the official description of wetlands in chapter 1, the soil labeled as hydric exhibits these qualities. It is black, mucky, smelly, rich in organic matter, and either periodically or perpetually saturated. Only hydrophytic plants, with specially adapted root systems, can survive in them. Imagine that houseplant soil on a large scale, and you'll see the long-term effects flooding can have on your garden soil. Keep in mind that saturation is not always indicated by standing water visible on the surface, because it can occur from beneath, with a rising water table. Often the saturation cannot be verified unless you dig a hole to reveal wet muck deeper down. During periods of high rainfall or flooding elsewhere, the water table can be charged to such a degree that it rises to an abnormal elevation, even though conditions still appear dry on the surface.

Anaerobic soil conditions can also cause some chemical changes to soil minerals. **Denitrification**, the depletion of soil nitrogen, is common and further reduces soil fertility. Sulfur as well as iron, manganese, and other trace elements can also undergo chemical changes that create either extremely depleted or toxic conditions, unhealthy for most types of plant life.

With all these changes occurring while the soil is underwater, it's wise to consult the experts on how best to nurture damaged soil before taking any radical steps. The most inexpensive and widely available resource is the USDA Soil Conservation Service. Their field agents are highly experienced in this problem and will suggest measures you can take. For example, if there is a chance of algae-cemented surface layers, they may recommend rototilling, disking, or ripping before you replant. Fertilizers may also be called for, and the agents' knowledge of special blends and application rates makes selection both more accurate and effective.

PLANT DAMAGE

Much of the serious flooding experienced in the United States occurs in the spring following ice- and snow-melt, or during the summer months, when slow-moving thunderstorms drop huge amounts of water in a short time. In both cases, temperatures are warm and plants are actively growing, which places them in a vulnerable position. Winter flooding is less damaging because plants are then dormant and require very little oxygen. But if flooded during summer, even cranberries, which spend much of their winter under-water, will suffer.

≣≣≣≣≣≣≣≣≣≣≣≣≣≣≣≣≣≣≣≣≣≣≣≣≣≣≣≣≣≣≣≣≣≣≣≣

The underground parts of most plants permeate a volume of soil as large as—or even larger than—the space occupied by the aboveground parts.

≣≣≣≣≣≣≣≣≣≣≣≣≣≣≣≣≣≣≣≣≣≣≣≣≣≣≣≣≣≣≣≣≣≣≣≣≣

As discussed above, the primary problem with saturated soils is the lack of oxygen, or anaerobic conditions. Plants carry on an active exchange of oxygen, called **respiration**, through both their roots and their leaves. Respiration is a critical component of plant growth; should there be an insufficient supply of oxygen in the root zone, respiration and growth slows or stops entirely. If the soil is saturated, there is resistance in the roots that inhibits the intake of soil nutrients. And when toxic gases such as ethylene accumulate, they will directly stop the growth and function of roots with which there is contact. All three of these factors—reduced respiration, limited nutrient uptake, and root death—occur when soil is saturated from a high water table or when covered with flood water.

The ultimate result of saturated soil is root death. Depending on the plant, the time of year, and the period of inundation, either part or all of the root system will die. You may have seen a plant wilt while standing in wet ground, which seems odd since it is receiving more than enough water. But what is really causing the wilt is root death, which prevents the uptake of enough water to support the foliage. There is no way to resurrect these roots and keep the leaves alive, although heavy pruning can reduce the foliage's water demand and perhaps save the plant if the soil dries out soon enough. But in most cases the plant is sure to die sooner or later.

Whenever a plant manages to survive summer flooding, unless it is a hydrophyte, it has probably experienced some root death. If there is only partial root death, an equal portion of the aboveground part of the plant will die, too. It reduces the demand on a recovering plant to remove these wilted limbs in order to ensure that sufficient moisture is transferred only to the limbs sure to survive.

Another method to help smaller plants survive is to draw the water away from the root zone. This is based on the concept that water always flows from an area of greater concentration to an area of lesser concentration. To take advantage of this principle, dig a shallow trench around the outside of the dripline, which is defined as the outer limits of the foliage canopy. This way you do not dig into the primary rooting area.

When you dig that circular trench, the water that had accumulated around the most important rooting area will flow out of the soil to gather in the trench. Frequently bail the water out of the trench to keep the flow going, because water will seep from the outside soil mass as well. Granted, this is far from efficient, but as yet there are no viable alternatives.

Tips on Helping Flooded Plants Recuperate

Flood waters, particularly those of high velocity in flash flooding, can be devastating to landscape plants. Imagine each plant as a stationary object that must bear the incredible weight and pressure of a large volume of flowing water. Twigs and branches too weak for the strain are torn away, and sometimes the trunk or stem breaks off at ground level. When the waters recede and you are faced with the remains of a plant, remember that there's a good chance it will recover.

At the end of a long, brutal winter, there is a tendency to go out and promptly cut down trees and shrubs because the damaged portions are so ugly to look at. The problem is that some plants *temporarily* defoliate in bitter cold but promptly leaf out again in spring. If the tree is cut down too early, it has no chance to exhibit the true degree and permanence of winter damage.

This is similar to what happens to flood-damaged plants. In fact, those that have broken off at the soil surface may return with incredible vigor, just as hard pruning can revitalize old woody shrubs. If some of the twigs and branches remain, it's a good idea to go out and clip off the tips because ragged tear wounds provide a better avenue for disease to enter the plant than clean cuts. Also clip off any limbs that are bent or broken, so that new, healthier growth will develop as a replacement.

Larger plants and stiff-trunked trees also suffer strain under fast-moving water. This strain is increased when debris collects on the upstream side of the trunk, sometimes accumulating into a large volume of material. The larger this volume, the more resistance it presents to moving water, with the loading entirely placed upon the tree trunk and the holding power of the roots. If the load is too great, the tree trunk breaks off, or there is tearing of the roots that are sustaining the most pressure. This loosens the anchorage of the tree on the upstream side, allowing the tree to lean but not lose its footing entirely. After the flood it is sometimes possible to straighten a leaning tree, but this should not be attempted without the assistance of a certified arborist. An arborist will assess the tree's health, projected longevity, and degree of damage and determine whether it is worth straightening or saving at all. If there is a chance of salvage, keep in mind that mature trees are extremely heavy; if the job isn't done correctly, serious damage can result.

The effects of erosion on plants works two ways: Either silt has built up around the plant and buried the bottom aboveground portions, or the original soil around the trunk and upper root system has been scoured away. Silt buildup is a problem for most woody plants because the bark beneath this deposit will rot if covered with soil. The technical term for this is **crown rot**. If the rot rings the main trunk, all food and water movement in the cambium layer is cut off, and the plant promptly dies. It is important to remove this silt buildup as soon as possible before rot begins to set in. This is essential in warm-season flooding, as plants are actively growing and rot begins quickly in such humid conditions.

If there is a single task you do in your landscape after a flood, let it be inspection of the bases of stems and trunks of all woody trees, shrubs, and vines. Remove the silt down to the pre-flood level of the soil, and the plants should recover beautifully.

≡≡≡≡≡≡≡≡≡≡≡≡≡≡≡≡≡≡≡≡≡≡≡≡≡≡≡≡≡≡≡≡≡≡≡≡≡≡≡

There are many woody plants that *do not* suffer from crown rot because they have evolved to thrive in flood plains. Alder, willow, cottonwood, and many others that are hydrophytes or display similar characteristics can send out roots anywhere along the trunk, branches, and twigs. In contrast, typical woody plants can never alter their bark to put out roots and suffer from even the most shallow burial with silt.

≡≡≡≡≡≡≡≡≡≡≡≡≡≡≡≡≡≡≡≡≡≡≡≡≡≡≡≡≡≡≡≡≡≡≡≡≡≡≡

Scouring is discussed in detail in chapter 5; basically, it is water erosion that digs out the soil. Scouring often exposes the roots of plants, which will quickly dehydrate once the water recedes. If there is only slight uncovering of the roots, some may develop bark and adapt naturally. In fact, this is how trees on the banks of streams can survive having their roots exposed from seasonal high water scouring away the soil. But plants sensitive to root exposure may not be so resilient, and if a larger portion of the rootball is uncovered, death can follow quickly. Therefore, it is essential to treat all plants as though they are the most sensitive: Get their roots covered up as quickly as possible. Be sure to seek the *original* soil level on the trunk to eliminate any chance of crown rot.

Flood water can be brutal on landscaping, especially when there has been scour erosion, which leaves mounds and cavities. Draining now to the center of a lot or away from drainage structures will cause serious problems in the future. Large-scale grading by heavy equipment, or smaller efforts by hand, may be required to smooth the property and make sure it has proper drainage gradients. However, it's best to avoid this grading until after you have cleaned up all the debris left behind by the floods. You may find everything from tires to entire trees littering the site, and even more stuff can be buried beneath the silt. These objects, if large enough, can become a hazard to equipment and could leach toxins into the surrounding soil for years to come.

It helps the yard drain better if you dig a few shallow trenches to carry away the water, but try to keep them far enough away from plants so their roots aren't damaged. Trenches are particularly valuable if a low spot is completely saturated and unlikely to drain on its own. A system of trenches can be used to drain water out of the surface of the soil when sensitive ornamental plants are suffering from a saturated, oxygenless root zone.

Flood Water Importation

Flood water typically originates in one place and flows downhill in its ultimate goal of reaching the sea, sometimes traveling hundreds of miles. During this long trip, it scours the soil, picking up all kinds of things from both the surface and newly exposed strata. Debris can range from entire tree trunks to microscopic organisms. Two of the most dangerous are the germs of notorious plant diseases and pieces of invasive plants, which can take root and grow wherever they settle out.

Water is the most efficient means of spreading soil-borne plant diseases from one place to another. Flood waters cover a tremendous amount of ground, and their muddy color is proof of their great ability to pick up and move just about anything. Imagine the exposure of 1 gallon of rainwater generated by a storm in Iowa as it travels to the Mississippi River Delta in the Gulf of Mexico. Diseases prevalent at any point of the watershed can move with the flood, and those inhabiting the soil survive best in water. Although there may be rigorous state inspections of produce shipped on interstate highways, flood waters far surpass them as an uncontrollable vector for disease.

Among the best known in the agricultural world are tobacco black shank fungus and many other species of the genus *Phytophthora*. Perhaps the most dreaded is *Phymatotrichum omnivorum*, the root rot afflicting plants in the southwestern states. Since these are fungi, they might not afflict plants right away. Soil fungi have microscopic, filamentous bodies, which spread out like spider webs in the earth. They must grow large enough to encounter the root system of a plant before it will be infected.

Other microscopic organisms may be transported by flooding but do not become active until the soil dries out again. These may be further transported on winds. Flood water that has run through cities may pick up a wide assortment of additional diseases dangerous to humans and animals, as well as plants. This is why there is great emphasis on the potential for contamination from mud deposited in flooded homes. Just as you are careful about contacting that mud, the garden soil is likely to be fairly contaminated for a while after a flood. Wear gloves and tall rubber boots to reduce your exposure when digging out garden plants.

Farmers have known for a long time that weed seeds are transported to their fields through irrigation ditches and similarly in flood waters. This was of great concern because many species of weeds also carry with them diseases that threaten crops. For example, the nightshades carry mosaic virus, and wild mustard can infect cabbage plants with club root. Weeds also harbor insect pests, which reproduce upon certain species of plants and then infect crops. Weeds can also be poisonous to both humans and livestock, and if they are transported onto your homesite, they can develop into colonies. Some of the most common are bracken fern, nettle, poison ivy or oak, poison hemlock, jimson weed, deadly nightshade, and foxglove.

Due to the presence of water during the summer months, rank-growing weeds grow prolifically on ditch banks, their flower stalks hanging over the water, where the seeds eventually fall. One study determined that several million weed seeds were found to pass a given point on a 12-foot ditch within a period of just 24 hours. These are the worst kind of plants to have introduced into a home landscape, yet this is exactly what happens on a larger scale when flooding occurs.

Many weed seeds are light and fluffy or covered with an oily film to make them float on top of the water. These are the most likely to be washed into a smaller flood and deposited elsewhere. Those weeds infecting rice fields and thriving in wet ground are a particular problem because they will literally thrive in the muck following long-term inundation. Because rice must be flooded for part of its growing season, these weeds are a burden to farmers, who today use special herbicides to control them. However, you'll see them growing en masse along the raised checks and roadsides wherever rice is grown. Secondly, many are exotic plants, not native to the United States or even North America. These have come here and invaded the countryside due to their tenacious and prolific character, and thus are likely to show up in your neighborhood or yard after a flood.

It's important to pay attention to what plants spring up in your yard during the first few seasons after a flood. Herbaceous weeds, runner grasses, reeds or cane, fast-growing vines, and rank-suckering trees are all difficult to control once established. Your diligence in spotting these invaders and your efforts to remove them will pay off in the long run, perhaps saving you from the perpetual chore of controlling tenacious species in the future. Refer to the plant lists in chapter 9 for noxious and invasive species to watch out for.

9

PLANTS FOR WET GROUND AND FLOOD PLAIN LANDSCAPING

Ask anyone involved in the creation or restoration of wetlands, and they will agree there are serious difficulties planting in an environment subjected to seasonal flooding. Even if planting is completed, there are many factors influencing whether or not the plants survive and grow vigorously. If you have experienced flooding in the past, you're probably aware of some of these problems; if not, it's important to know what they are and how they influence planting in wetlands and flood plains.

1. Depth to Water Table

As described in earlier chapters, the water table is the elevation of underground water, at what point you would encounter it if digging a hole. The water in many lowland areas can be just inches from the soil surface, while not far away it can be much deeper down. This influences planting because in high water table conditions, there is very little soil available that is properly aerated. As a result, many plants will be forced to root only in this thin aerated layer, and rootballs of larger species take on a pancake-like shape. Any attempts at deeper rooting will encounter anaerobic conditions, where root tips promptly rot. Species of plants that are either hydric or semihydric, however, send roots down below this dry layer into the wet. In fact, most grow best under these conditions.

> Pancaked root systems of trees can be a serious hazard. This flat rooting has very little holding power, even when the trees are perfectly healthy. High winds can topple these trees without warning, and if they are close to homes, damage could result. Be aware of tree species not adapted to wet ground because these are the most likely to have this limited rooting ability.

To resolve any doubts about the actual depth of your water table, if you suspect it is unusually shallow, dig a hole during the summer months to see for yourself. If your water table is high, larger plants, such as trees and sizable shrubs, will suffer most from limited root space. This doesn't mean you can't have trees; it only limits you to species better adapted to wet ground. Herbaceous perennials with shallow roots are also good candidates, along with many annuals. Of course, lawn and prairie wildflower-grass mixes are ideal. Prairie grasses and others used in livestock pastures have an expansive root system, which helps hold your surface soil if the yard is flooded. Many of them are capable of surviving even after being underwater for 4 or 5 days, and their holding power will reduce the need for grading and filling after flooding.

2. New Planting and High Water

Managers of flood plain parks perpetually grapple with the effects of high water upon newly planted trees, shrubs, and grasses. This is a serious difficulty where high water occurs annually. The flowing water will yank the rootballs right out of the ground since the roots have not had time to work their way into the surrounding soil for anchorage. This shows just how ineffective planting from container-grown stock can be if flooding is regular. Intermittent flooding may allow 1 to 3 years for the plants to become established, but even then, depending on typical velocity, there still may not be enough holding power in the rootball. Soil conditions—either too dense to penetrate or too sandy to remain intact—compound this problem.

Ecologists have developed a number of ways to stabilize plants in their revegetation projects. One choice is planting from seed, as is done with oak trees in hardwood bottomlands. Oaks and other taprooted species send out a long, anchoring taproot before there is much top growth, a mechanism ideal for holding a seedling against moving water. However, if sprouted in a container, this taproot distorts almost immediately; when planted out, it is unlikely to be stable enough to withstand the flow of water. Better success can be obtained with bare-root deciduous plants because the root systems, although limited, are not formed into the shape of a container. Bare roots stand a better chance of survival, depending on how many seasons pass before they must contend with high water.

Another method utilizes unrooted cuttings anchored sometimes 3 feet deep in the soil. A great deal of success in parks has been obtained this way. Only certain easily rooted species will tolerate this kind of treatment, but it is the ideal means of establishing shade trees in flood plains. (More information on these techniques are detailed below in the discussion of willows and poplars.)

3. Rabbit and Rodent Predation

The expression "breeding like rabbits" is, of course, well grounded in fact. Rabbits and many species of rodents breed very quickly, and their populations can become abnormally high. But even with normal population densities, they are perpetually hunting for food. These animals not only eat green shoots of seedlings, they will literally destroy any vegetation in their territory during winter or other times when food is scarce. Even the bark of young trees is at risk, particularly during winter.

The best way to protect young seedlings, container plants, and bare-root cuttings is with tubular shelter devices. One commonly used in reforestation consists of a tubular net of rigid polymesh. It is **photodegradable**, so sunlight will cause it to disintegrate after a number of years, by which time the plant no longer requires such protection. The tube is only about 4 inches in diameter and about a foot tall, anchored in place by a 3-foot stake. These are limited but effective. The landscape industry has developed larger shelter tubes of solid, translucent plastic about 3 feet tall. Ideal for reducing sunscald on sapling trunks, they also deny larger animals, such as beavers, access to the young, tender bark. These are widely available from garden centers.

You can also create your own protective devices with what scrap materials you have on hand, particularly hardware cloth or aviary wire, as both have very small openings. Ranchers have been barricading their sapling trees this way for years to keep them safe from browsing livestock. The key is to be sure there are no openings large enough for field mice, which does limit your options, and the base of the shelter should be partially buried to keep them from squeezing in underneath. Stakes can be anything from the steel posts for electric fence to bamboo or hardened-off suckers cut from last year's winter pruning. Although shelters can increase resistance to flowing water if the site does flood, they do have a limited ability to protect the bark from gouges by floating debris.

4. Competing Weeds

In chapter 3 we looked at how weeds can be imported onto a site by flood waters. This presents a problem because many species are quick to sprout from seed; if allowed to survive through their first season in your landscape, chances are they will be there to stay. Some, such as Bermuda grass, are valued for their soil-stabilizing effects, but a single fragment of root or stolon can develop into a sizable patch. Unless dealt with immediately, it will invade your entire landscape; with each flood, it will become even more widespread. Controlling such plants may become the bulk of your maintenance effort.

NATIVE PLANT Species occurring naturally in a region

EXOTIC PLANT Species not a natural part of the ecosystem, imported from elsewhere

Ecologists revegetating wetlands find one of the most difficult issues to be invasion by exotics. Ideally, their goal is to keep a site limited to plant species native to that regional ecosystem. There is a great emphasis on revegetating with native grasses, but we must always remember that the reason the natives are no longer generally around is that exotic species came into the picture at some point and crowded them out. Therefore, a site revegetated exclusively with natives will suffer continual invasions of exotic species, a fact that stymies ecologists and motivates armies of volunteers and students to go out and weed newly restored wetland projects. When the exotics are rank-growing vines that blanket large areas, such as Japanese honeysuckle or kudzu, they can literally smother huge tracts of land.

PLANTING TECHNIQUES FOR HIGH WATER TABLES

In many residential flood plain landscapes, poor drainage, dense soil, and a very high water table make it difficult to create an attractive garden. Whenever there is a problem soil of any type, the most reliable solution is to plant in earth raised up above the existing soil. We can take inspiration from farmers in the Mississippi Delta, who have always faced problems with saturated field conditions. They developed a method of plowing that creates long rows of mounded soil for planting. This allows the majority of the roots to remain in the drier soil of the mound while still accessing moisture below. Even some Native American cultures that inhabited flood plains raised their living areas by mounding earth by hand over many generations.

This example shows how the levee and floodwall systems can be combined to protect homesites located close to creeks or streams. Inside, only two walls of landscape timbers were needed to create a sizeable raised planter, which backed up to a corner in the floodwall. Because this planter was inside a floodwall and would not be required to stand in flood water, it could be constructed of timbers. Of further interest in this scenario is that the addition of an earth berm on the outside of the floodwall helps to stabilize the banks of the creek so that erosion will not cause undercutting of the wall foundation. Undercutting can disturb the proper loading forces needed for cantilever floodwalls and can seriously destabilize gravity walls. (US Army Corps of Engineers, National Floodproofing Committee)

These raised planters are built in separate modules with a concrete block core, stucco finish, and bull-nosed brick caps.

Raised Planters

Gardens should follow this example by being planted in raised areas. They can be constructed in different ways, depending on budget, space, and availability of materials. Where recurring flooding is expected, masonry or concrete are the only viable materials that can stand up to the debris loads and scouring and resist floating. It is important to have a professional design any raised planters within a flood area because special footings may be required to resist disturbance by the loading forces of water.

The ideal choice for a raised planter is poured concrete, which requires extensive forming and is not particularly attractive. When veneered with stone or brick, though, it can become an important visual element in the landscape. Where floodwall protection is in place on a homesite, locating raised planters to use the floodwall on one or more sides cuts down on construction costs. Walls can also be constructed of masonry block with decorative facing or of structural bricks, both of which contain hollow cells. The cells are essential because they provide places for steel reinforcing bar to be built into the wall, which ties it together and increases structural strength. However, it is essential that all the cells, particularly those large ones in concrete blocks, be completely filled with concrete for maximum reinforcement.

A double tier series of planters helps to take up grade to this elevated house pad. The wall core is either poured concrete or block with stone veneered on the outside.

Walls made entirely of field stone do not have this strength, because the irregular shapes do not allow steel reinforcing bar to be easily incorporated into the wall. Where stone appearance is desired, it's best to build the wall with a block or concrete core, then veneer it with stone.

Raised planters must always be constructed with some means of drainage, or water will fill the planter when it rains, or even after regular watering. **Weep holes**, commonly built along the bottom of masonry planter walls, allow water to seep out for no additional construction cost. When they drain onto paved surfaces, however, they may cause staining or slippery algae buildup. Another option is to install a perforated pipe or gravel French drain tied into an opening in the wall where water may flow out. Do this before filling the planter with soil.

Any time you build a masonry wall and fill it with soil, there will be some moisture absorption into the porous mortar, blocks, or concrete. The moisture travels through, gradually picking up minerals and lime, all of which end up as crystals on the outside face of the wall. This white efflorescence is unsightly and may have to be removed with muriatic acid if it defaces the masonry. Sealing the inside walls of the planter before it is filled with soil can help reduce this problem. Sealing compounds, such as inexpensive asphalt emulsion or some of the newer, paint-on waterproofing products, are all effective if applied evenly and thick enough to do the job.

Brick is an affordable and attractive veneer material for planter walls, but it can be structural too. You'll know structural brick from common brick because there is a series of holes that are made to accommodate reinforcing steel bars.

Where the soil is poor or the ground too soggy, lawns too can be raised up for better success with turf grass. This 18-inch-high wall was constructed of formed concrete that allows for clean, modern curves in the walls. The walls can be painted, veneered, or left as is.

As long as you are building a raised masonry planter, make it about 18 inches tall, and it can double as outdoor seating. If you use a rowlock course of brick or other material to widen the top, it will be much more comfortable to sit upon.

Wood is not a suitable building material for flood-prone sites. It may cost less in both materials and labor, but in damp climates wood planters can be very short-lived. And with the cost of lumber rising dramatically, it may not remain economical for long. The best wood products for a wet site are railroad ties, which are heavily treated with creosote and other preservatives.

Besides the tendency to rot, one real problem with using wood in flood plains is its natural buoyancy. Unless very well anchored in a strong footing, anything constructed of wood could literally float away. Plus, creosote-laden railroad ties, splintery surfacing, or narrow walls do not present an inviting place to sit. Many people are also concerned with the toxicity of wood preservatives, which can leach out into the soil or drain into natural wildlife areas.

Mounding

During the 1970s, mounding in gardens became the rage for both planting areas and lawns. The flat look was out, and a more undulating, irregular ground plain was in. Even today there are still many unsuccessfully designed and executed examples of old mounding in residential landscapes. However, mounding re-mains the most inexpensive choice for flood plain gardening, and it can be very successful if you follow the proper design guidelines.

New types of interlocking structural blocks such as these make building raised planters a home improvement project. Designed so that portions of the block "key" into other blocks eliminates the need for steel reinforcing, and the blocks themselves have attractive split-face finishes.

Locating where the mounds are to be created in the landscape should be done carefully because they can act like small-scale levees to block drainage. A mound can cause inaccessible pockets at the back of a lot that are virtually impossible to dry out. Also, take into consideration where water will flow when it runs down off the mound, particularly if it is a sizable area and sprinklers are involved. If done properly, you can solve the wet soil problem and improve your overall drainage at the same time. To be on the safe side, buy an hour of time with a professional, either a landscape architect, landscape contractor, architect, building contractor, or civil engineer, to help with the particulars. Hauling in soil can

Earth mounds can be very attractive ways to landscape when boulders are used to break up the smooth surface. A variety of boulder sizes provide the best effect. Decorative stream beds, either dry or as a water feature, make these raised plantings a central focus of the garden.

be quite expensive and mound-building labor-intensive, so a mistake can be very difficult to resolve after the mounds are in place.

There are rules about landscape mounds, just as there are strict guidelines for the creation of a levee. Both should be built up in layers, with each layer properly compacted to avoid uncontrolled settling later on. But while levees are straight and even in their shape, mounds should appear more natural, with soft, undulating curves. If you feel unsure how this should look, study some natural ranges of hills or mountains for their irregularity and proportions of height and mass. For a large project it may be helpful to bring in a landscape designer to guide you in laying out the size, shape, and location of each mound.

In terms of gradients, topographical landscape maps show a contour line for each foot of rise on a slope. Rise divided by the distance of the slope equals a percent slope. For example, 1 vertical foot of rise in 2 horizontal feet of run is a 50% slope. When shaping a mound the sides should *never* be steeper than 1 foot of rise to 3 feet of run, or about a 30% slope. They can and should be less than this gradient, if space and available fill material permit.

The ultimate goal of this kind of earthwork is to provide a place for *plants* to grow. To do so they require water, which tends to run off steeper slopes more quickly than it can be absorbed into the soil. Therefore, the more gradual the side slopes of your mound, the better they will support plants. The top of the mound should not be pointed or ridged, because this is not suitable for absorbing water. Make it flat and slightly rounded so you can grow many plants here, as it is the best portion of the mound as far as plants are concerned. Plants on the side slopes should be able to hold the soil to reduce the potential for erosion. If there is flooding and the top of the mound is still above the waterline, the side slopes will take a beating from wave action. The more vegetation you have growing upon them, the less erosion that will occur, particularly if the plants have large, fibrous root systems.

Planting on the side slopes should also be done carefully to avoid two problems that can result from flood conditions. First, the outside edge of the rootball can be exposed as the soil washes away. Second, there must be a means of collecting water to feed the plant adequately. If you are using landscape boulders, these can be "planted" into the side of the mound where they act as retaining devices. Plants can be set in the areas just above boulders, where they will remain fairly stable.

This mound with boulders and a waterfall is completely cloaked in plants. This kind of protection is ideal for mound planting in flood plains with soil holding species on the sides and wetland plants in the moist, low areas.

Lowland gardening can still be very attractive. Combining iris, hostas, and unusual bog perennials, beautiful gardens should not be viewed as unrealistic.

If you aren't using rock in the mound, you can kill two birds with one stone by carving out a little bench for each plant on the side of the mound and set the soil aside. Then dig the planting hole on the inside edge of the bench. Use this excavated soil to cover up the rootball. Build a big, strong berm on the outside rim and pack it down tightly. It should confine all the water without washing out. Eventually, as the plant grows older, it won't be so dependent on this watering basin, which early on is essential.

Good Plants for Lowland Gardens

If you have constructed raised planters or mounds to keep plants well above wet ground, most plants will grow without any problem, but their size should be in proportion to that of the bed. For example, if you place a taprooted tree into a mound only 3 feet tall, that taproot will quickly grow deep, beyond the benefits of the higher ground, and still suffer from rot. A tree or shrub too large at maturity for a masonry planter is likely to crack the walls and make them highly vulnerable to collapse under flood conditions. Reserve these raised planting areas for your favorite perennials, roses, or flowering vines.

When we consider plants for lowland homesites, you'll find there are these groups:

1. Natives that normally occur in wetland habitats and that are also suitable for landscaping.

2. Exotic newcomers originally introduced as crops or landscape plants but have also proved well adapted to wetlands.
3. Versatile native and exotic species occurring in *both* wetlands and upland areas.

It can save a lot of money in dead plants if you know which species are most likely to survive on a flood-prone site. To begin with, following are lists of native trees and shrubs recognized as members of wetland ecosystems and widely used in restoration of sites. After that are more general lists of native and exotic species that should be successful in wet ground. However, just as there are many kinds of wetlands, there are also many kinds of wet ground, some highly saturated, others only periodically soggy. You should expect some trial and error before you find out which ones do best at your site. Keep in mind that if certain native plants grow wild around your home, chances are they will grow equally well in your landscape. Best of all, most natives are well adapted to your climate, have some pest-resistant qualities, and require no special care.

The US Fish and Wildlife Service has prepared a document, *National List of Plant Species That Occur in Wetlands,* with compilations of both natives and exotics that serve as indicator species to help determine whether a wetland exists. Many are so widely adapted that they can grow just about anywhere. Because this manual lists only genus and species names, with no common names, it's too technical for most folks, but it has become the definitive resource used by all agencies in wetland identification. To purchase a copy of either the regional or the national summary, contact the USDA Soil Conservation Service.

Native Wetland Trees and Shrubs

Many of these species are widely used in landscaping and available from most nurseries. They are alphabetized by common names, which are more widely recognized than the botanical names.

Common name	Botanical name
Conifers	
Atlantic White Cedar	*Chamaecyparis thyoides*
Bald Cypress	*Taxodium distichum*
Black Spruce	*Picea mariana*
Northern White Cedar	*Thuja occidentalis*
Pond Pine	*Pinus serotina*

Tamarack	*Larix laricina*
Western Red Cedar	*Thuja plicata*

Broadleaf Trees

American Elm	*Ulmus americana*
Balsam Willow	*Salix pyriolia*
Bebb Willow	*Salix bebbiana*
Black Ash	*Fraxinus nigra*
Black Tupelo	*Nyssa sylvatica*
Black Willow	*Salix nigra*
California Sycamore	*Platanus racemosa*
Carolina Ash	*Fraxinus caroliniana*
Coastal Plain Willow	*Salix caroliniana*
Dahoon	*Ilex cassine*
Eastern Cottonwood	*Populus deltiodes*
Elderberry	*Sambucus canadensis*
Green Ash	*Fraxinus pennsylvanica*
Honey Locust	*Gleditsia triacanthos*
Laurel Oak	*Quercus laurifolia*
Loblolly-bay	*Gordonia lasianthus*
Mountain Alder	*Alnus tenuifolia*
Nutmeg Hickory	*Carya myristiciformis*
Overcup Oak	*Quercus lyrata*
Pawpaw	*Asimina triloba*
Pin Oak	*Quercus palustris*
Poison Sumac	*Toxicodendron vernix*
Possumhaw	*Ilex decidua*
Pussy Willow	*Salix discolor*
Red Alder	*Alnus rubra*
Redbay	*Persea borbonia*
Red Maple	*Acer rubrum*
Red Osier Dogwood	*Cornus stolonifera*
River Birch	*Betula nigra*
Sandbar Willow	*Salix exigua*
Silver Maple	*Acer saccharinum*
Southern Bayberry	*Myrica cerifera*
Speckled Alder	*Alnus rugosa*
Sugarberry	*Celtis laevigata*
Swamp Chestnut Oak	*Quercus michauxii*
Swamp Cottonwood	*Populus heterophylla*
Swamp Privet	*Forestiera acuminata*
Swamp White Oak	*Quercus bicolor*
Sweetbay Magnolia	*Magnolia virginiana*

Southern magnolia (Magnolia grandiflora) is a mainstay of gardens below the Mason-Dixon line. They are more tolerant of wet ground than most evergreens and offer attractive glossy foliage with large white flowers.

Bog garden with pink flowers.

Many of the southern oaks (Quercus spp.) are native and have evolved to thrive in wet ground. Although it takes a century to reach this size, oaks make fine shade trees both reliable and widely available at nurseries. Rosedown plantation.

Sycamore	*Platanus occidentalis*
Water Elm	*Planera aquatica*
Water Hickory	*Carya aquatica*
Water Oak	*Quercus nigra*
Water Tupelo	*Nyssa aquatica*
Willow Oak	*Quercus phellos*

Shrubs

Bog Rosemary	*Andromeda glaucophylla*
Great Laurel	*Rhododendron maximum*
Highbush Blueberry	*Vaccinium corymbosum*
Labrador Tea	*Ledum groenlandicum*
Leatherleaf	*Chamaedaphne calyculata*
Sheep Laurel	*Kalmia angustifolia*
Swamp Rose	*Rosa palustris*
Sweet Pepperbush	*Glethra alnifolia*
Ti Ti	*Cyrilla racemiflora*
Winterberry	*Ilex verticillata*

Ornamental Trees, Shrubs, and Vines for Wet Ground

Tolerance of saturation varies according to duration, season, and depth. **Spp.** indicates multiple species of that genus are included. This is to provide a guideline for identifying the most water-tolerant groups of plants. This table includes native and exotic species.

Botanical name	Common name	Evergreen or Deciduous
Trees		
Acer spp.	Maples	D
Alnus spp.	Alders	D
Amelanchier canadensis	Serviceberry	E
Betula spp.	Birches	D
Carpinus caroliniana	American Hornbeam	D
Casuarina spp.	Beefwoods	E
Celtis spp.	Hackberries	D
Cornus florida	Flowering Dogwood	D
Crataegus phaenophyrum	Washington Hawthorn	D
Eucalyptus citriodora	Lemon-Scented Gum	E
Eucalyptus robusta	Swamp Mahogany	E
Eucalyptus rudis	Flooded Gum	E
Fagus grandifolia	Beech	D
Fraxinus latifolia	Oregon Ash	D
Fraxinus pennsylvanica	Green Ash	D

Ilex opaca	American Holly	E
Ilex verticillata	Winterberry	E
Larix laricina	American Larch	D
Liquidambar styraciflua	Sweetgum	D
Magnolia grandiflora	Southern Magnolia	E
Magnolia virginiana	Sweetbay Magnolia	D/E*
Melaleuca quinquenervia	Cajeput Tree	E
Myoporum laetum	Myoporum	E
Nyssia sylvatica	Sour Gum	D
Pinus elliottii	Slash Pine	E
Pinus glabra	Spruce Pine	E
Pinus rigida	Pitch Pine	E
Pinus strobus	White Pine	E
Pinus taeda	Loblolly Pine	E
Platanus acerifolia	London Plane Tree	D
Platanus racemosa	California Sycamore	D
Populus spp.	Poplars	D
Prunus serotina	Black Cherry	D
Quercus spp.	Southern Oaks	D
Rhus spp.	Sumacs	
Roystonea spp.	Royal Palms	E
Sabal palmetto	Cabbage Palm	E
Salix spp.	Willows	D
Sambucus spp.	Elderberries	D
Sassafras albidum	Sassafras	D
Sorbus americana	American Mountain Ash	D
Ulmus americana	American Elm	D

*depends on climate

Shrubs and Vines

Alnus rugosa	Speckled alder	D
Andromeda polifolia	Bog Rosemary	E
Aronia arbutifolia	Chokeberry	D
Aronia melanocarpa	Black Chokeberry	D
Bignonia capreolata	Cross Vine	E
Calycanthus spp.	Spice Bushes	E
Cephalanthus occidentalis	Buttonbush	E
Chamaedaphne calyculata	Leatherleaf	E
Clethra acuminata	Ninebark	D
Clethra alnifolia	Sweet Pepperbush	D
Cornus spp.	Dogwoods	D
Gaultheria shallon	Salal	E
Gelsemium rankinii	Swamp Jessamine	E
Hamamelis spp.	Witch Hazels	D

Sweetgum (Liquidambar styraciflua): *These beautiful trees are native to our bottomland hardwood forests and their color stands out boldly in autumn. Sweetgum tends to grow narrowly upright in cultivated landscapes, but in the wild they are more round-headed and irregular.*

Sycamores (Platanus spp.) *are also called plane trees and were used in ancient Greece to shade their outdoor universities. They are popular street trees with symmetrical growth and attractive buff-colored bark. Western natives such as California sycamore have more irregular shapes than their eastern cousins and make more casual landscape trees.*

The variegated box elder (Acer negundo 'Variegatum') *has become a favorite landscape tree due to the creamy tint of the two-toned leaves. It is just one of the many types of maples that thrive in lowlands offering a good choice of fall color, form, and sizes.*

There are a number of different species of poplar (Populus spp.), *or cottonwood, native to river bottoms from coast to coast. Ideal for planting from unrooted poles, they root quickly and do not mind periodic flooding. In fact, these are excellent all-purpose trees for every situation, from bank stabilization to shading.*

QUICK PICKS ON WET-GROUND OAKS AND WILLOWS

Quercus falcata—Cherrybark Oak
Quercus laurifolia—Laurel Oak
Quercus lyrata—Overcup Oak
Quercus michauxii—Swamp White Oak
Quercus nutallii—Nutall Oak
Quercus shumardii—Shumard Oak
Quercus virginiana—Live Oak
Salix alba—White Willow
Salix babylonica—Weeping Willow
Salix blanda—Wisconsin Weeping Willow
Salix caprea—Goat Willow
Salix discolor—Pussy Willow
Salix matsudana 'Navajo'—Globe Navajo Willow
Salix matsudana 'Tortuosa'—Corkscrew Willow
Salix purpurea—Purple Osier Willow
Salix viminalis—Osier Willow

Ilex glabra	Inkberry	E
Illicium floridanum	Florida Anise	E
Illicium parviflorum	Ocala Anise	E
Itea ilicifolia	Hollyleaf Sweetspire	E
Kalmia microphylla	Western Laurel	E
Leucothoe spp.	Leucothoes	E
Lindera benzoin	Spicebush	D
Myrica spp.	Wax Myrtles, Bayberries	E
Osmanthus americana	Devilwood	E
Rosa palustris	Swamp Rose	D/E
Rubus spp.	Blackberries	D/E
Salix spp.	Willows	D
Thuja occidentalis	American Arborvitae	E
Vaccinum spp.	Huckleberries, Blueberries	E
Viburnum spp.	Viburnums	E/D
Zenobia pulverulenta	Andromeda	E

Ornamental Perennials for Water Gardens, Wetlands, and Soggy Soils

Botanical name	Common name	Type	Flower color†
Acontium spp.	Monkshood, Wolf's Bane	Perennials	B, W, Y
Agapanthus spp.	Lily of the Nile	Perennials	B, W
Ajuga spp.	Carpet Bugle	Perennial Groundcovers	B
Alocasia	Elephant's Ear	Foliage, Tropical	No
Aster spp.	Michaelmas Daisy	Perennials	Many
Astilbe spp.	False Goat's Beard	Perennials	Many
Caltha palustris	Marsh Marigold	Semiaquatic Perennial	Y
Canna generalis	Canna	Perennial	Many
Centranthus ruber	Red Valerian	Perennial	P
Colocasia esculenta	Taro	Foliage, Tropical	Rare
Echinacea purpurea	Purple Coneflower	Perennial	P
Eichhornia crassipes*	Water Hyacinth	Aquatic Flower	L
Galium odoratum	Sweet Woodruff	Perennial Groundcover	W
Hemerocallis	Daylily	Perennial	Many
Hibiscus moscheutos	Rose Mallow	Perennial	R, P, W
Hosta spp.	Hostas	Perennials	B, W
Iris spp.	Japanese Irises, Siberian Irises	Perennials	Many
Lobelia cardinalis	Cardinal Flower	Perennial	Scarlet
Lythrum virgatum*	Purple Loosestrife	Perennial	Purple
Mentha spp.	Mints	Perennial Herbs	W, B
Mimulus spp.	Monkeyflowers	Perennials	R, O, Y, P
Monarda didyma	Bee Balm	Perennial	R, P
Myosotis scorpioides	Forget-Me-Not	Perennial/ Annual	B
Phormium tenax	New Zealand Flax	Lily	Rare
Physostegia virginiana	Obedient Plant	Perennial	W, P
Primula spp.	Primroses	Perennials	P, W, B
Rodgersia spp.	Rodgersias	Perennials	W
Sanguinaria canadensis	Bloodroot	Perennial	W, P
Soleirolia soleirolii	Baby's Tears	Perennial Groundcover	No

Elephant's ear (Alocasia) is an easily recognized subtropical foliage plant that relies on a unique root system, which can obtain oxygen out of the air when the roots are saturated. Easy to grow, it is a striking addition to any tropical garden.

Daylilies (Hemerocallis) have been hybridized into hundreds of different flower colors and are a reliable perennial for all but the coldest climate zones. They are an excellent source of flowers in soggy gardens and are easily divided into new plants when they develop into sizeable clumps.

There are a variety of different hybrid calla lilies (Zantedeschia) today but none of them reach the size of this, the common calla. They ask for little except plenty of water and morning sun and make excellent cutting flowers.

Phormium tenax: The leaves of this foliage plant can be green, variegated, or bronze depending on the cultivar. The plants can grow to well over six feet tall and when mature they flower with exotic spikes that rise up out of the leaves and attract hummingbirds galore. It is also quite resistant to heat and direct sunlight.

A mass of chain ferns crowds this boggy low spot in the garden, but not all fern species can take this type of wet ground.

Solidago spp.	Goldenrods	Perennials	Y
Trollius spp.	Globe Flowers	Perennials	W, Y, O
Zantedeschia spp.	Callas	Perennials	W, P, L, Y

*This species tends to invade native ecosystems and should be used with care.

†Flower colors: B—blue, L—lavender, O—orange, P—pink, R—red, W—white, Y—yellow; Many—range of colors; Rare—rarely flowered.

Irises for Bogs and Marshes

Irises have long been favorite marginals of water gardens because of their stately form and vivid flower colors. **Marginals** are plants clustered around the edges of the water, where its depth may fluctuate with the seasons. These are not to be confused with Dutch irises or German bearded irises, which require well-drained—sometimes even arid—conditions. Many species of marginal irises originated in Asia. The Japanese *kaempferi* tolerate standing water far better than others and are found naturalized alongside rice crops in Japanese and Chinese paddies, which are flooded during the summer

Marginal bog iris live around the edges of ponds where the waterline is likely to fluctuate a bit. They produce luscious flowers with large, flat petals.

and drier through the winter months. This preference for wet summer conditions makes these irises ideal for flood plain landscaping and for making the fringes of ponds and wetlands brilliantly colorful. *Kaempferi* hybrids are also called "clematis-flowered irises" because the flowers resemble that popular group of vines. Masses of *kaempferi* have been likened to hordes of nesting butterflies, as the delicate flower petals so resemble them.

Popular Marginal Irises Each of these groups may offer dozens of hybrids in different colors. Listed below are just a few species of this extensive group of aquatic or bog and marsh plants.

Common name	Botanical name	Height (in.)	Water depth (in.)
Blue Flag Iris	*Iris versicolor*	24	6
Eolian	*Iris 'Eolian'*	42	6
Japanese Iris hybrids	*Iris kaempferi*	30	0
Louisiana Iris	*Iris "Louisiana hybrids"*	36	6
Red Iris	*Iris fulva*	24	6
Siberian Iris	*Iris siberica*	36	2
Yellow Water Iris	*Iris pseudacorus*	48	10

Ferns, Native and Exotic

Native ferns can be found inhabiting the damp, shady margins of wetlands and scattered through bottomland hardwood forests. Not all ferns tolerate wet feet, though; if you try planting the dryland species in wetlands, they will quickly rot and die.

Ferns are primitive plants with fairly shallow roots, making them a good choice for wet ground. The key is to keep them out of the hot afternoon sun to avoid unsightly brown, crispy edges on the leaves. Ferns also prefer consistent moisture year round, but some die back over the summer months in arid climates. Exotic ferns are also numerous, many of them frost-tender and thus best suited to temperate states.

The ferns listed grow in moist conditions, but those indicated with an asterisk (*) are the most tolerant of saturated ground and even standing water.

Common name	Botanical name
Autumn Fern	Dryopteris erythrosora
*Climbing Fern	Lygodium palmatum
*Chain Ferns	Woodwardia spp.
*Cinnamon Fern	Osmunda cinnamomea
Goldie's Fern	Dryopteris goldiana
Hart's Tongue	Phyllitis scolopendrium
Holly Fern	Cyrtomium falcatum
*Interrupted Fern	Osmunda claytoniana
Japanese Climbing Fern	Lybodium japonicum
*Japanese Painted Fern	Athyrium nipponicum
*Lady Fern	Athyrium filix-femina
Leatherleaf Fern	Rhumohra adiantiformis
Marginal Shield Fern	Dryopteris marginalis
*Marsh Fern	Thelypteris palustris
Maidenhair Ferns	Adiantum spp.
Ostrich Fern	Matteuccia struthiopteris
*Royal Fern	Osmunda regalis
Sword Fern	Polystichum munitum
*Toothed Wood Fern	Asplenium trichomanes
*Walking Fern	Camptosorus rhizophyllus

Ornamental Grasses and Sedges

One of the factors defining a specific type of wetland is the predominant vegetation, in a marsh typically consisting of reeds, canes, grasses, and sedges. Many, such as the ubiquitous cattail, will find their way into a new wetland so quickly they can become immediate pests. But with these early invaders under control, more variety in form and color adds interest to wet gardens. Due to the soil-holding characteristics of many, they provide the added benefit of better erosion control.

Beware of those identified with an asterisk, as these have proved to be overly aggressive in natural ecosystems and can be difficult to control once established.

Botanical name	Common name	Plant Type
*Arundo dondax	Giant Reed	Cane
Carex spp.	Sedges	Sedge
*Cortaderia selloana	Pampas Grass	Ornamental Grass
Cyperus spp.	Papyrus, Umbrella Grass	Ornamental Grass
Equisitum hyemale	Horsetail, Scouring Rush	Reed
Juncus effusus	Common Rush	Reed
Miscanthus spp.	Miscanthus Grasses	Ornamental Grass
*Phyllostachys spp.	Bamboos	Cane

Grasses Used to Revegetate Wetlands

Agrostis alba	Redtop
Agrostis stolonifera	Creeping Bentgrass
Agrostis tenuis	Colonial Bentgrass
Alopecurus arundinaceus	Creeping Foxtail
Echinochloa cursgalli	Japanese Millet
Festuca arundinacea	Tall Fescue
Festuca rubra	Creeping Red Fescue
Lolium multiflorum	Annual Ryegrass
Lolium perenne	Perennial Ryegrass
Panicum clandestinum	Deertongue
Panicum virgatum	Switchgrass
Phalaris arundinacea	Reed Canarygrass
Poa trivialis	Rough Bluegrass

Miscanthus (Miscanthus spp.) is just one species of the many ornamental grasses that are becoming popular garden plants in both wetland and dryland gardens.

IDEAL LANDSCAPE PLANTS OR NOXIOUS PESTS?

Perhaps the greatest threat to restoration of wetlands is invasion of exotic plants that not only crowd out natives but also prevent the proper succession. It is estimated that in California there are 1,025 different species of naturalized exotic plants, comprising more than 17 percent of the total flora. Mild-climate states experience similar invasions, particularly in the Deep South, where frost is less common. But this is not limited to the Sun

Belt, because 35 percent of all plant species in New York state are exotic.

For example, if a dense exotic running grass becomes well established at a site, it can be virtually impossible to control, as it breaks and roots so easily. The dense coverage of this mat of grass prevents taller weeds from growing, which would be nature's way of providing shade for new tree seedlings. With exotics as part of the equation, restoration of wetlands to their original state is difficult if not impossible; therefore, some ecologists are loosening up on their stringent demand for native species only. On the other hand, many wetland experts consider purple loosestrife a beautiful addition to American wetlands, even though it is native to Europe and highly invasive. Other species of loosestrife are native here and often present in wetlands, but few are as rugged as purple loosestrife. You may hear conflicting opinions about many such plants as the battle over vegetation is waged in the scientific arena.

The ornamental plants we value for their ability to survive in soggy ground are some of the worst invaders, a factor you must consider if you plant them anywhere near natural open space. This is not to say all are a problem in every case, because local climates and landscapes vary considerably. However, where invasive plants have become established, even the most antiherbicide people are willing to make an exception if poisoning invaders is the only hope for reclaiming our wetlands, dunes, and prairies.

Pampas grass (Cortaderia selloana) is most admired for its fluffy, white flower heads, but it can also become a pest plant because clumps are very large and dense. They are much like the native sawgrasses and can easily go wild, spreading quickly as the fluffy seeds travel a long way on the wind.

The Problem Children

Cytissus racemosus—**Scotch Broom, Shrub** A frequent problem in arid hill country, it may invade riparian forests and shrub swamps. It reproduces prodigiously from seed.

Lonicera japonica—**Japanese Honeysuckle, Vine** Botanists are horrified to discover that this well-loved honeysuckle sprouts readily from seed. In fact, there are so many seedlings each year, the plant is displaying an increased tolerance for cold. As a result, not only has it invaded forests and wetlands in southern states, it is advancing northward toward our hardwood forests. The plant shades out understory species and prevents tree seedlings from sprouting, ultimately destroying the ecosystem's ability to regenerate itself.

Bambusa, Phyllostachys **spp.—Bamboos, Canes** Bamboos have been the gardener's scourge since they were first introduced into cultivated landscapes. Incredibly rugged, they spread by underground rhizomes into huge, impenetrable stands. Once established, they are virtually impossible to eradicate without chemicals and a tremendous amount of labor. In wildlands it becomes a nightmare.

Scotch Broom (Cytissus racemosus).

Pueraria lobata—**Kudzu, Vine** There are many who would love to draw and quarter the individual who first introduced this rampant, woody, Asian vine into the southern states a century ago. What began as an experiment in alternative livestock forage went disastrously awry. That fateful day was followed by a plant invasion like none other, with a single vine capable of cloaking a mature tree in record time. Kudzu grows fast, is long-lived, and stops at nothing,

A bamboo thicket.

not buildings nor waterways nor fence lines. This new scourge of the South has naturalized and will become a serious obstacle in future wetland restoration.

Ailanthus altissima—**Tree of Heaven, Tree** Another Asian introduction, this tree grows into incredible thickets everywhere, in both overly wet and overly dry conditions.

Cortaderia selloana—**Pampas Grass, Grass** Huge mounds of this razor-edged grass, similar to swamp sawgrass but much bigger, can completely choke dry riverbeds in arid climates. Their rootballs are massive and dense, making them very difficult to control.

Other Overly Successful Plants
Artichoke Thistle
Arundo dondax—Giant Reed
Celastrus orbiculatus—Chinese Bittersweet
Wild Grapevines
Ligustrum spp.—Privets
Melia azedarach—Chinaberry Tree
Nut Sedge
Robinia pseudoacacia—Black Locust
Some perennial turf grasses

SAVE MONEY WITH WILLOWS AND POPLARS

The genus of cottonwoods, *Populus* obtained this name because it rooted so easily the entire population could successfully grow it. Willows likewise are very easy to grow, and both are backbone plants of many wetland ecosystems. Those who are involved in revegetation projects use both poplars and willows for holding disturbed soil and collapsing banks. These species root with a fine but dense network. If planted in a container, the roots tend to take that shape and are less adventurous when transplanted onto a wetland site. As a result, they do not take hold, and the plant is often whisked away with the first or second year of high water.

Through long-term trial and error, the greatest success has been achieved by planting unrooted, dormant, leafless sticks or poles straight into the ground. An 8-foot pole can be buried 3 feet deep; when flood waters rise, there is plenty of holding power, the only risk being pole breakage. This resistance to flood damage was proven in 1986 in the river bottom between levees on the Feather River in Northern California. Late in the autumn of 1985, 450 hybrid poplar (cottonless cottonwood) poles 8 feet long were planted in postholes 3-feet deep where no container-grown tree had ever survived the occasional high water. In February 1986 the river rose to 80 feet, completely covering the newly planted poles in a surging flood, but failing to dislodge them while breaking a levee farther downstream. When the water subsided, there was only about 5% loss of poles, primarily due to breakage caused by debris forced against the poles, which were barely an inch in diameter at their widest point.

To establish any species of these trees, such as corkscrew willow, weeping willow, Lombardy poplar, or the new hybrids, it is more successful, less expensive, and far easier to use dormant cuttings and poles. There has also been similar success with buttonbush (*Cephalanthus occidentalis*), red osier dogwood (*Cornus stolonifera*), and elderberry (*Sambucus canadensis*). If the soil is soft enough, you can push them in by hand, or try a bulb planter or posthole digger to dig a hole first. Cuttings should be planted as soon as possible after they are cut from either the branches or the stump suckers of a mother plant. They will strike root all along the buried portion of the cutting and show considerable growth in the spring.

The best way to hold stream embankments is with these cuttings. In chapter 2 there is a discussion of revetments and wattling, both effective means of stabilizing eroding slopes. Another simple method is to cut short segments and push them deep into the embankment, spacing them 12 to 18 inches apart. If there is a good chance of high water, cut long segments and push them into the bank as far as you can, then cut the ends off to a suitable length. Be sure to push them in bottom-first, as it can be difficult to tell. If you're lucky, the cuttings will strike root before the next high water and bind the soil within the first season. Other species aren't quite as willing to grow from cuttings, but if they are available, it's worth a try. Look for soft wood of sycamores, green ash, alders, and sweetgum.

For natural wetlands and water holes, take cuttings off local wild stock, the ideal species for your area. Few people realize that the very same species of wildflower, for example, can be different from region to region. This is because plants adapt to unique qualities of microclimates or soil types. Thus, local seed is more at home there than seed of the same species that originates elsewhere. In addition, cuttings and even container-grown plants brought in from somewhere else may have a tough time acclimating, a factor that may spell their demise over the long haul. This has been a problem for those restoring wetlands, because there isn't always enough parent stock available locally for a large project. Imported plants simply fail to thrive, as well as suffer in transit from the grower.

CHAPTER 10
SOURCES AND RESOURCES

University/County Cooperative Extension

Provides professional assistance, publications, and local programs. Nearby offices may be listed in the state government section of the phone book under headings such as "Farm Advisor."

Environmental Protection Agency (EPA)

Wetlands Hotline 1-800-832-7828
Call for information or to ask questions about wetlands.

Region I: CT, MA, ME, NH, RI, VT
Wetlands Protection Section
(WWP-1900)
US EPA—Region I
John F. Kennedy Federal Building
Boston, MA 02203-1911
(617) 565-4421,
FAX (617) 565-4940

Region II: NJ, NY, PR, VI
Wetlands Protection Section
(2WM-MWP)
US EPA—Region II
26 Federal Plaza, Rm. 837
New York, NY 10278
(212) 264-5170, FAX (212) 264-4690

Region III: DE, MD, PA, VA, WV
Wetlands Protection Section (3ES42)
US EPA—Region III
841 Chestnut Street
Philadelphia, PA 19107
(215) 597-9301, FAX (215) 597-1850

Region IV: AL, FL, GA, KY, MS, NC, SC, TN
Wetlands Regulatory Section
US EPA—Region IV
345 Courtland Street N.E.
Atlanta, GA 30365
(404) 347-4015, FAX (404) 347-3269

Region V: IL, IN, MI, MN, OH, WI
Wetlands and Watersheds Section
(WQW-16J)
US EPA—Region V
77 West Jackson Boulevard
Chicago, IL 60604
(312) 886-0243, FAX (312) 886-7804

Region VI: AR, LA, NM, OK, TX
Wetlands Protection Section (6E-FT)
US EPA—Region VI
1445 Ross Avenue, Suite 900
Dallas, TX 75202
(214) 655-2263, FAX (214) 655-7446

Region VII: IA, KS, MO, NE
Wetlands Protection Section (ENRV)
US EPA—Region VII
726 Minnesota Avenue
Kansas City, KS 66101
(913) 551-7573, FAX (913) 551-7863

Region VIII: CO, MT, ND, SD, VT, WY
Wetlands Protection Section
(8WM-WQ)
US EPA—Region VIII
999 18th Street, 500 Denver Place
Denver, CO 80202-2405
(303) 293-1570, FAX (303) 391-6957

Region IX: AZ, CA, HI, NV, Pacific Islands
Wetlands and Coastal Planning Section (W-7-4)
US EPA—Region IX
75 Hawthorne Street
San Francisco, CA 94105
(415) 744-1971, FAX (415) 744-1078

Region X: AK, ID, OR, WA
Wetlands Section (WD-128)
US EPA—Region X
1200 Sixth Avenue
Seattle, WA 98101
(206) 553-1412, FAX 206 553-1775

United States Army Corps of Engineers
Division Offices—
Regulatory Program

US Army Corps of Engineers
Lower Mississippi Valley Division
(CELMV-CO-R)
P.O. Box 80
Vicksburg, MS 39180-0080
(601) 634-5818

US Army Corps of Engineers
Missouri River Division
(CEMRD-CO-R)
P.O. Box 103, Downtown Station
Omaha, NE 68101-0103
(402) 221-7290

US Army Corps of Engineers
New England Division
(CENED-OD-P)
424 Trapelo Road
Waltham, MA 02254-9149
(617) 647-8057

US Army Corps of Engineers
North Atlantic Division
(CENAD-CO-OP)
90 Church Street
New York, NY 10007-9998
(212) 264-7535

US Army Corps of Engineers
North Central Division
(CENCD-CO-MO)
536 South Clark Street
Chicago, IL 60605-1592
(312) 353-6379

US Army Corps of Engineers
North Pacific Division
(CENPD-CO-R)
P.O. Box 2870
Portland, OR 97208-2870
(503) 326-3780

US Army Corps of Engineers
Ohio River Division (CEORD-CO-OR)
P.O. Box 1159
Cincinnati, OH 45201-1159
(513) 684-3972

US Army Corps of Engineers
Pacific Ocean Division
(CEPOD-CO-O)
Building 230
Fort Shafter, HI 96858-5440
(808) 438-9258

US Army Corps of Engineers
South Atlantic Division
(CESAD-CO-R)
Room 313
77 Forsythe Street SW
Atlanta, GA 30335-6801
(404) 331-2778

US Army Corps of Engineers
South Pacific Division (CESPD-CO-O)
630 Sansome St., Room 1216
San Francisco, CA 94111-2206
(415) 705-1443

US Army Corps of Engineers
Southwestern Division
(CESWD-CO-R)
1114 Commerce Street
Dallas, TX 75242-0216
(214) 767-2432

United States Fish and Wildlife Service

Regional Offices
Headquarters, US Fish and
Wildlife Service
Department of the Interior
1849 C Street NW
Washington, DC 20240

Region 1: CA, HI, ID, NV, OR, WA
US Fish and Wildlife Service
Eastside Federal Complex
911 NE 11th Avenue
Portland, OR 97232-4181
(503) 231-6118

Region 2: AZ, NM, OK, TX
US Fish and Wildlife Service
500 Gold Avenue, SW
Albuquerque, NM 87103
(505) 766-2321

Region 3: IL, IN, IA, MI, MN, MO, OH, WI
US Fish and Wildlife Service
Whipple Federal Building
Fort Snelling, MN 55111-4056
(612) 725-3563

Region 4: AL, AR, FL, GA, KY, LA, MS, NC, SC, TN
US Fish and Wildlife Service
1875 Century Boulevard, #410
Atlanta, GA 30345-3301
(404) 679-4000

Region 5: CT, DE, MA, MD, MA, NH, NJ, NY, PA, RI, VT, VA, WV
US Fish and Wildlife Service
300 Westgate Center Drive
Hadley, MA 01035-9589
(413) 253-8200

Region 6: KS, MO, NE, ND, SD, UT, WY
US Fish and Wildlife Service
134 Union Boulevard
Lakewood, CO 80228
(303) 236-7920

Region 7: Alaska
US Fish and Wildlife Service
1011 East Tudor Road
Anchorage, AK 99503
(907) 786-3542

United States Department of Agriculture Soil Conservation Service (SCS)

Each state has its own SCS office. It is listed in your telephone book under "U.S. Government, Department of Agriculture." Following are the main regional offices.

West National Technical Center
Federal Building, Room 248
511 N.W. Broadway
Portland, OR 97209-3489
(503) 326-2824

South National Technical Center
Building 23, Room 60
501 Felix Street
Fort Worth Federal Center
P.O. Box 6567
Fort Worth, TX 76115
(817) 334-5253

Midwest National Technical Center
Federal Building, Room 152
100 Centennial Mall North
Lincoln, NE 68508-3866
(402) 437-5346

Northeast National Technical Center
160 East Seventh Street
Chester, PA 19013-6092
(215) 499-3979

Federal Emergency Management Agency (FEMA)

Regional Offices

Region I: CT, ME, MA, NH, RI, VT
FEMA Region I
J. W. McCormack POCH, Room 442
Boston, MA 10219-4595
(617) 223-9561

Region II: NJ, NY, PR, VI
FEMA Region II
26 Federal Plaza, Room 1337
New York, NY 10278-0002
(212) 225-7202

Region III: DE, DC, PA, VA, WV
FEMA Region III
Liberty Square Building, 2nd Floor
105 South Seventh Street
Philadelphia, PA 19106-3392
(215) 931-5750

Region IV: AL, FL, GA, KY, MS, NC, SC, TN
FEMA Region IV
1371 Peachtree Street, N.E., Suite 700
Atlanta, GA 30309-3108
(404) 853-4400

Region V: IL, IN, MN, OH, WI
FEMA Region V
175 West Jackson Boulevard, 4th Floor
Chicago, IL 60604-2698
(312) 408-5533

Region VI: AR, LA, NM, OK, TX
FEMA Region VI
Federal Regional Center, Room 206
800 N. Loop 288
Denton, TX 76201-3698
(817) 898-5127

Region VII: IA, KS, MO, NE
FEMA Region VII
911 Walnut Street, Room 200
Kansas City, MO 64106-2085
(816) 283-7002

Region VIII: CO, MT, ND, SD, UT, WY
FEMA Region VIII
Building 710, Box 25267
Denver Regional Center
Denver, CO 80225-0267
(303) 235-4830

Region IX: AZ, CA, HI, NV
FEMA Region IX
Building 105
Presidio of San Francisco
San Francisco, CA 94129-1250
(415) 923-7176

Region X: AK, ID, OR, WA
FEMA Region X
Federal Regional Center
130 228th Street S.W.
Bothell, WA 98021-9796
(206) 487-4862

FREE GOVERNMENT PUBLICATIONS

Write or call the nearest FEMA, Corps of Engineers, USDA SCS, or EPA office to obtain any of the following informative publications. Also available are numerous brochures that condense these books into handy references.

FEMA Publications

Attn: Publications
Federal Emergency Management Agency
P.O. Box 70274
Washington, DC 20024

FEMA-234	*Repairing Your Flooded Home*
FEMA-14	*Guide to Flood Insurance Rate Maps*
FEMA-15	*Design Guidelines for Flood Damage Reduction*
FEMA-54	*Elevated Residential Structures*
FEMA-55	*Coastal Construction Manual*
FEMA-85	*Manufactured Home Installation in Flood Hazard Areas*
FEMA-102	*Floodproofing Non-Residential Structures*
FEMA-114	*Design Manual for Retrofitting Floodprone Residential Structures*
FEMA-116	*Reducing Losses in High-Risk Flood Areas: A Guidebook for Local Officials*
FIA-12	*Appeals, Revisions, and Amendments to Flood Insurance Maps: A Guidebook for Local Officials*
FIA-13	*Flood Emergency and Residential Repair Handbook*
FIA-2	*Answers to Questions About the National Flood Insurance Program*

US Army Corps of Engineers Publications

Local Flood Proofing Programs, June 1994, National Flood Proofing Committee

Flood Proofing Systems & Techniques, December 1984, Flood Plain Management Services Program

EPA Publications

Livestock Grazing on Western Riparian Areas, Ed Chaney et al.

OTHER PUBLICATIONS ON WETLANDS

Private Wetlands Conservation Corporations These organizations are especially dedicated to public education and recognition of wetlands as a national resource.

Trout Unlimited
1500 Wilson Boulevard, Suite 310
Arlington, VA 22209-2310
(703) 284-9409

Ducks Unlimited, Inc.
Ducks Unlimited is a private, nonprofit organization dedicated to conserving wetland habitat for waterfowl and other wildlife. Open membership is $20.00 a year. It is an excellent example of how sportsmen have become deeply involved in wildlife conservation, and the group is responsible for many large wetland restoration projects across the nation. Although many of the members hunt waterfowl in season, a good number of nonhunters join Ducks Unlimited due to the longstanding reputation of this group. Following are the Ducks Unlimited regional offices.

Western Region
9823 Old Winery PL, #16
Sacramento, CA 95827-1720
(916) 363-8257

Great Plains Region
3502 Franklin Avenue
Bismarck, North Dakota 58501
(701) 258-5599

Southern Region
101 Business Park Drive #D
Jackson, MS 39213
(601) 956-1936

Further Reading from Environmental Specialists

agAccess—The Agricultural
Information Source
P.O. Box 2008
Davis, CA 95617
(916) 756-7177
Free book catalog.
Carries a wide assortment of agricultural and environmental books from different publishers. Selected titles follow.

Earth Ponds: The Country Pond Maker's Guide, T. Matso, $16.95.

Better Trout Habitat: A Guide To Stream Restoration & Management, C. J. Hunter, $24.95.

Adopting a Wetland, Steve Yates, $5.95.

Island Press—The
Environmental Publisher
Box 7
Covelo, CA 95428
(800) 828-1302
Free catalog.
One of the most well respected publishers of environmental books, Island also distributes environmental books by other national publishers.

Wetland Creation and Restoration, Jon A. Kusler & Mary E. Kentula, eds., Island Press.

Creating Freshwater Wetlands, Donald Hammer, Lewis Publishers, $66.00.

Wetlands Planting Guide for the Northeastern United States, Gwendolyn Biggs, Environmental Concern, $19.95.

Wetlands, William Mitsch & James Gosselink, Van Nostrand Reinhold, $64.00.

Freshwater Marshes: Ecology and Wildlife Management, Milton Weller, University of Minnesota Press, $34.95 hardcover, $16.95 paperback.

Everglades: The Ecosystem and Its Restoration, Steve Davis & John Ogden, eds., St. Lucie Press, $97.50.

Terrene Institute Book Catalog
1717 K. Street, NW
Washington, DC 20006
(202) 833-8317

Lake Smarts: The First Lake Maintenance Handbook, Steve McComas, $18.95 paperback.

Clean Water and Productive Rangelands, Susan V. Alexander, $6.95 paperback.

Other Books on Wetlands, Flooding, and Gardening

Attracting Birds to Southern Gardens, Thomas Pope, Neil Odenwald, & Charles Fryling, Jr., Taylor Publishing.
How to identify birds, know their needs, and encourage them into gardens or natural wetland habitats.

The Audubon Society Nature Guides: Wetlands, William A. Niering, 1985, Alfred A. Knopf.
The ultimate field guide to wetlands of midwest, eastern, and deep southern states. Neglects western states.

Environmental Overkill, Dixy Lee Ray & Lou Guzzo, Harper Perennial Books.
A glimpse at the politics behind wetland issues, it discusses questions regarding the scientific foundations of many government programs.

Gardening With Native Plants of the South, Sally Wasowski & Andy Wasowski, Taylor Publishing. A good resource for better understanding of many native wetland species and how to grow them successfully.

List of Plant Species That Occur in Wetlands, US Fish and Wildlife Service. Individual Regions 1 through 9, and California, Alaska, Caribbean, and Hawaii. Prices vary from $14.95 to $19.95.
National summary $25.95.
Available from:
Superintendent of Documents
US Government Printing Office
Washington, DC 20402
(202) 512-1800
Call for current prices and shipping.

Planet Earth—Flood, Champ Clark, 1982, Time-Life Books. A graphic view of flood events around the world.

The Southern Gardener's Book of Lists, Lois Trigg Chaplin, Taylor Publishing. Good resource for plants suited to wet ground, heavy clay, and Louisiana gumbo soil.

SOURCES OF AQUATIC AND WETLAND PLANTS, SEED, AND SUPPLY

American Aquatic Gardens
621 Elysian Fields
New Orleans, LA 70117
(504) 827-0889

Environmental Concern, Inc.
210 West Chew Avenue
P.O. Box P
St. Michaels, MD 21663

Forest Farm
990 Tetherow Road
Williams, Oregon 97544-9599
Carries a broad selection of native trees and shrubs for wetlands.
Catalog $3.00.

Jungle Laboratories
P.O. Box 630
Cibilo, TX 78108
(512) 658-3503

Pond Doctor
HC65, Box 265
Kingston, AR 72742
(501) 665-2232

Kesters Wild Game Food Nurseries, Inc.
P.O. Box V
Omro, WI 54963

Siskiou Rare Plant Nursery
2825 Cummings Road
Medford, OR 97501-15241
(503) 772-6846
Catalog $2.00.

Southern Tier Consulting
45 South Main Street
P.O. Box 610
Portville, NY 14770
(716) 968-3120
Free catalog.

Van Ness Water Gardens
2460 North Euclid
Upland, CA 91786
(714) 982-2425
Catalog $3.00.

Wildlife Nurseries
P.O. Box 2724
Oshkosh, WI 54903

Lilypons Water Gardens
6800 Lilypons Road
Lilypons, MD 21717-0010
(301) 874-5133
Color catalog $5.00.

Glossary

Anaerobic A condition in which oxygen is absent.

Aquatic plant A species that grows in or on the water.

Aquifer A body of rock or soil that is sufficiently porous and permeable to be useful as a source of water.

Base flood elevation The elevation establishing the 100-year flood on Flood Insurance Rate Maps.

Borrow area An area where material has been excavated for use as fill at another location.

Check valve A type of valve that allows water to flow one way but automatically closes when water attempts to flow the other direction.

Closure A shield made of strong material, such as steel, aluminum, or plywood, used to temporarily fill in a gap in a flood wall, levee, or sealed structure left open for day-to-day convenience, such as access to doors and driveways.

Crawl space Low space below the first floor of a house, where there has not been excavation deep enough for a basement, but where there is often access for pipes, ducts, and utilities.

Debris impact load Sudden load induced on a structure by debris carried by flood water.

Design flood Commonly meaning the magnitude of flooding used as a standard for design of homes and other structures within a flood plain.

Dry floodproofing A method used in areas of low-level flooding to completely seal a home against water.

Ecosystem A system made up of a group of living organisms and their physical environment, and the relationships between them.

Elevation The raising of a structure to place it above flood waters on an extended support structure.

Exotic Plant or animal life not native to the region, country, or continent.

Fen A type of wetland whose primary source of soil saturation is alkaline groundwater.

Fill Material such as earth, clay, or crushed stone dumped in an area and compacted to increase the ground elevation.

Flash flood A flood that reaches its peak flow in a short length of time (hours or minutes) after the storm or other event causing it. It is often characterized by high-velocity flows.

Flood A partial or complete inundation of normally dry land areas from overland flooding of a lake, river, stream, ditch, or other body or channel.

Flood crest The maximum stage or elevation reached by the waters of a flood at a given location.

Flood duration The length of time a stream is above flood stage or overflowing its banks.

Flood frequency A statistical expression of the average time period between floods equaling or exceeding a given magnitude.

Flood fringe The portion of the flood plain that lies beyond the floodway and serves as a temporary storage area for flood waters during a flood. This section receives water that is shallower and of lower velocity than that of the floodway.

Flood Hazard Boundary Map (FHBM) The official map of a community that shows the boundaries of the flood plain and designates special flood hazard areas. It is superseded by the Flood Insurance Rate Map after a more detailed study has been completed.

Flood Insurance Rate Map (FIRM) The official map of a community prepared by FEMA that shows the base flood elevation, along with special hazard areas and the risk-premium zones for flood insurance purposes. Once it has been accepted, the community is part of the regular phase of the NFIP.

Flood Insurance Study A study performed by any of a variety of agencies and consultants to delineate the special flood hazard areas, base flood elevations, and risk-premium zones. The study is funded by FEMA and is based on detailed site surveys and analysis of site-specific hydrologic characteristics.

Flood plain The relatively flat area or lowland adjoining a watercourse or a body of standing water, and that has been or may be covered by flood water.

Floodproofing Any combination of structural and nonstructural additions, changes, or adjustments to properties and structures to reduce or eliminate flood damage to land, water and sanitary facilities, structures, and contents of buildings.

Floodwall A barrier constructed of resistant material, such as concrete or masonry block, to keep water away from a structure.

Flood warning The issuance of information about an imminent or current flood.

Flood watch Flooding is possible in a designated watch area.

Freeboard A factor of safety expressed in feet above a design flood level, used to compensate for unknown factors that could flood design height, such as wave action or obstruction of the floodway.

Hydric soil A soil saturated, flooded, or ponded long enough during the growing season to develop anaerobic conditions in the upper part.

Hydrophyte Any plant growing in a soil or substrate that is at least periodically deficient in oxygen as a result of excessive water content.

Hydrodynamic loads Forces imposed on an object, such as a structure, by water moving around it. Among these loads are positive frontal pressure, drag effect along the sides, and negative pressure on the downstream side.

Hydrostatic load Force imposed on a surface, such as a wall or a flood slab, by a standing mass of water. The water pressure increases with the square of the water depth.

Levee A barrier of compacted soil designed to keep flood water away from a structure.

100-year flood A flood having an average frequency of occurrence on the order of once in 100 years, although the flood may occur in any year.

Peat Partially carbonized organic matter found in bogs.

Pier An upright support member of a building, functioning as an independent structural element in supporting and transmitting building loads to the ground.

Pile An upright support member of a building, usually long and slender in shape, driven into the ground by mechanical means. Piles often cannot act as individual support units and require bracing to other pilings.

Retrofitting Floodproofing measures taken on an existing structure.

Riparian The area adjacent to a stream or body of water that is at least periodically influenced by flooding.

Riprap Broken stone, cut stone blocks, cobble, or rubble placed on slopes to protect them from erosion or scouring caused by flood waters or wave action.

Scouring The erosion, or washing away, of slopes or soil by high-velocity water.

Seepage The passage of water through a porous medium, such as an earthen embankment or a masonry wall.

Silt Sediment of fine mineral particles and organic matter carried in fast-moving water.

Slab on grade A structural design where the first floor sits directly on a poured concrete slab that sits directly on the ground.

Special flood hazard area Portion of the flood plain subject to the 100-year flood, also known as Zone A.

Underseepage Seepage along the bottom of a structure, floodwall, or levee, or through the layer of earth beneath it.

Velocity The rate or speed that water flows, usually expressed in feet per second. 1 foot per second is equivalent to about 0.7 miles per hour.

Watershed An area that drains to a single point. In a natural basin this is the area contributing flow to a given place or stream.

INDEX

Note: **Boldface** page references indicate illustrations and captions.

A

Acer negundo 'Variegatum', **145**
Ailanthus altissima, 153
Algae, **62,** 66–67, 123–24
Alocasia, **148**
Anaerobic soil, 123, 124, 125
Animals, wetlands and, 45–55, 57, 59–60, 66–68
Aquifer, 43

B

Bald eagles, **65**
Bamboo, 153, **153**
Bambusa, 153, **153**
Banks of streams and rivers, preservation of, 31–38, **35–38**
Base flood, definition, 22
Base flood elevation
    definition, 22, 104
    floodproofing and, 101, **101–3,** 104
Bats, 67
Beavers, **47,** 68
Berms, for floodproofing, **105–6,** 105–7, 109
Biobarrier, 121
Birds, **50,** 57, 59–60, 63, **64–65,** 67
Bogs, 49
Boil order, 94
Boils, 12–13, **12**
Bottomlands, 49
Box elder, variegated, **145**
Brush, for streambank preservation, 36–37, **36**
Buildings, damaged by flooding, **92,** 93

C

Calla lilies, **148**
Cats, 53–54, 66
Chimneys, 13
Cholera, flooding and, 90
Clay sinker, 68
Climax species, 48
Coastal flooding, **15**
Colonizing species, 48
Concrete
    for raised planters, 135
    sacked, 35, **35**
Cortaderia selloana, **152,** 153
Coyotes, **65**
Creeks, 23–38. *See also* Streams
Creep, 75
Crown rot, 127
Croxen, Fred, 28
Culverts, 37–38, **37,** 117
Cytissus racemosus, 152, **153**

D

Daylilies, **148**
Deltas, subsidence in, **43,** 44
Denitrification, 124
Digging out. *See* Emergency procedures and digging out
Disaster plan, 86–89
Ditch drains, 115–18
Diversion ditches, 121
Documents, preserved during flood, 88
Dogs, 53
Drainage in wet soils, 111–12
    concepts underlying techniques, 114
    questions for homeowners, 112–13
    structures for, 113–15, **116, 120, 122**
    ditch drains and swales, 115–18

169